Auschwitz Children and Mengele Experiments The Immoral and Atrocious Research on Children in the Auschwitz Concentration Camp During World War II

Jack Stew Barretta

Published by vincenzo nappi, 2021.

AUSCHWITZ CHILDREN AND MENGELE EXPERIMENTS THE IMMORAL AND ATROCIOUS RESEARCH ON CHILDREN IN THE AUSCHWITZ CONCENTRATION CAMP DURING WORLD WAR II

First edition. September 18, 2021.

ISBN: 979-8215199732

Written by Jack Stew Barretta.

Also by Jack Stew Barretta

The Black Death and The Medical Practice How The Plague Pandemic Influenced Medicine and Surgery
The Black Death and his Unexpected Positive Consequences to Society
Auschwitz Children and Mengele Experiments The Immoral and Atrocious Research on Children in the Auschwitz Concentration Camp During World War II

Table of Contents

AUSCHWITZ CHILDREN AND MENGELE EXPERIMENTS

The Immoral and Atrocious Research on Children in the Auschwitz Concentration Camp during World War II

By

Jack Stew Barretta

CHAPTER I

THE NAZI DOCTORS AND THE THIRD REICH

Many doctors in Germany were convinced that they were the chosen people to create a healthy, racially pure *Volkskörper* (body of people) and by doing so, establishing a racial utopia. As strong supporters of National Socialism, they welcomed the founding of the Third Reich. After Hitler acceded to power, German physicians joined the SS in particular. During the twelve years of the Nazi era, seven percent of German doctors became members of the SS. The average membership of the population was only 0.6 percent. Moreover, doctors were also overrepresented as a profession, with teachers consisting less than half a percent and musicians only three percent. Only lawyers had a larger share in the SS than doctors.

Historian Michael Kater explains the large share of doctors in the SS by the fact that Himmler especially recruited 'social and professional elites', such as lawyers and doctors, and that the SS offered them 'professional and socioeconomic security and desired recognition'. The doctors realized that the SS offered them limitless control over life and death, which would command more respect for their profession and themselves.

The average income of German doctors extremely increased after 1933, even exceeding the income of lawyers. The Nazi doctors of the human experiments also joined the SS in large numbers. German doctors were far more reluctant to join the NSDAP than the SS. Before 1933, only seven percent of all German doctors joined the NSDAP (Nazi party). They joined the party when it seemed opportune to do so, in 1933, and particularly in 1937. In 1933, physicians consisted almost a quarter of all academic professionals in the NSDAP. Most doctors joined the

NSDAP in 1937, with a membership rate of 43 percent of the total profession. German physicians sat on the fence during the first years of the Nazi era, insecure about the effects of the new regime on their profession. By 1937, the Third Reich had won their trust for several reasons. The NSDAP had solved the economic crisis and had reorganized the medical profession. Moreover, the regime had solved "the Jewish question" in the medical sector. Jews were overrepresented as physicians during the Weimar Republic. The Völkischer Beobachter (official newspaper of the Nazi Party) stated on 23 March 1933:

> *There is probably no job that is so important for the greatness and future of the nation as the medical one. [...] But no one is as Jewish as he is and so hopelessly in foreign matters Thinking has been drawn into it. Jewish lecturers dominate the chairs of medicine, de-soul the healing art and have with generation after generation of young doctors soaked in mechanistic spirit. Jewish 'colleagues' headed the Professional associations and medical associations; they falsified and undermined the medical concept of honor native ethics and morals.*

The Nazi regime took measures to solve the "Jewish problem" in the medical profession. In the summer of 1933, 235 scientists and researchers were fired at German universities for being non-Aryan or Marxists, many of whom were Jews.

In 1934, the regime imposed restrictions on the medical profession, excluding Jews from their jobs. They could hardly practice as family doctors anymore and were fired en masse at hospitals and universities. The exclusion of Jews created job opportunities for German physicians.

The Nazi doctors all had their own reasons to join the NSDAP and the SS. However, ideological support and careerism are the most important reasons. In all cases, it was an interaction between these two motivations; nevertheless, the career opportunities that the Third Reich offered were for most of them decisive. A few examples will illustrate this point. After his participation in the Beer Hall Putsch (which was a failed coup d'état by Nazi Party leader Adolf Hitler), Gebhardt refrained from politics and concentrated on his career. In May 1933, he contacted his old childhood friend Himmler. They had lost contact in 1923. When they met again in 1932, Himmler promised Gebhardt that he could work as a physician in his personal staff. In a letter of May 1933, Gebhardt asked for Himmler's support. The letter shows that 'Gebhardt, as a staunch National Socialist, was ambitiously striving to become something in the state.'

At this time, Gebhardt was head of the Institut für Leibesübungen in Berlin-Charlottenburg. Gebhardt initially wanted to join the SA (*Sturmabteilung* was the Nazi Party[1]'s original paramilitary[2] wing. It played a significant role in Adolf Hitler's rise to power[3] in the 1920s and 1930s) out of careerism, but Himmler prevented him from doing so since this would damage his career. Instead, Gebhardt joined the SS in May 1933. He did not join from an ideological perspective but solely out of careerism.

The second person that serves as an example is Mengele. He joined the SA in November 1933. However, he had already left the organization within one year by October 1934, because membership of the SA was no longer in the interest of his career after the Night of the Long Knives (was a purge that took place in Nazi Germany from June 30 to July 2, 1934. Chancellor Adolf Hitler, urged on by Hermann Göring and Heinrich Himmler, ordered a series of political extrajudicial executions intended to consolidate his power and alleviate the concerns of the German military about the role of Ernst Röhm and the Sturmabteilung

---

1. https://en.wikipedia.org/wiki/Nazi_Party

2. https://en.wikipedia.org/wiki/Paramilitary

3. https://en.wikipedia.org/wiki/Adolf_Hitler%27s_rise_to_power

(SA), the Nazis' paramilitary organization, known colloquially as "Brownshirts.". He did not join the NSDAP until 1937, since he wanted to focus on his studies. It remains unclear to what extent he supported National Socialism and anti-Semitism.

He joined the NSDAP and the SS out of ideological support for National Socialism and careerism. He joined both organizations after he had finished his studies and started to build his career in medicine. For Mengele, being a young scientist in eugenics and heredity, membership was necessary to get a position at universities or research institutes.

The physicians and National Socialists developed similar perspectives on the creation of a German state based on racial purity. The doctors perceived themselves as social engineers and they knew the new state would need them to accomplish their racial goals, as is demonstrated in the previous chapter. Once the Third Reich was established, the doctors realized that through collaboration they could improve their social status. This higher social status was created by the special position of doctors within the National Socialist state, and the rapid ascension within the academic world because of the exclusion of Jewish colleagues. Therefore, it has become clear that opportunism is the main motive for the doctors' membership in the SS and NSDAP.

For the Nazi doctors who committed human experiments, The Third Reich improved their social status and career because of the special status doctors had within the new state. However, we can observe two patterns about the generations of the Nazi doctors.

First, only the older physicians, born before 1900, were appointed as professors during the Third Reich. All of them received their professorships during the years 1935-1937. The exclusion of Jews paved the way for this group to become professors. Gebhardt became an extraordinary Professor in Sports Medicine at the University of Berlin in 1935.

Second, the group of younger doctors, born after 1900, built their careers in the Third Reich mainly out of their SS-membership. They finished their medical studies in the 1930s. Because these young physicians had only recently received their doctoral degrees, they obviously lacked the scientific experience to become professors. Nevertheless, the Third Reich offered them unlimited possibilities for promotion and a higher social status. Seemingly, the outbreak of the war drifted them away from their scientific careers. They had to serve in the army or the SS during the first years of the war. Nevertheless, the expansion of the SS and the concentration camp system offered them an unprecedented way to further their scientific careers. The National Socialist dictatorship offered members of this generation particular benefits: on the one hand, the Nazi dictatorship undoubtedly increased the pressure on young to adapt Academics, if they were planning a professional career in Germany and not emigration thought of putting themselves at the service of the regime. On the other hand, that meant Destruction of the rule of law, civil society, and moral barriers in the scientific research and practice an enormous Mephistophelian opening of the A horizon of possibilities that these young, radical academics in particular are not unaffected by let.

The outbreak of the Second World War was crucial to the careers of the Nazi doctors. The war demanded research that would improve German warfare and combat the negative consequences of the war, such as injuries, illnesses, and epidemics. The concentration camps became filled with "inferior", degenerated people that could be used as research subjects. The camps offered opportunities for academic purposes, such as research for the Habilitation or a scientific publication, enabling physicians to teach in medical faculties or even to become professors.

However, how did the Nazi doctors end up working on the experiments in the concentration camps? Three avenues can be distinguished: doctors who had positions within the SS or concentration camps and were assigned or ordered to execute the experiments; doctors who were recruited by the Nazi authorities based on their previous research; and doctors who contacted the SS at their own initiative. The institutes and organizations that ordered or supported the experiments were crucial to the execution of the experiments and the allocation of doctors to the concentration camps.

The group that was assigned or ordered to execute or participate in the experiments is the largest group of these perpetrators. This group can be divided into doctors who were originally employed as doctors at the concentration camps, and doctors who were sent to the camps with the assignment to execute the experiment. Nevertheless, once assigned, almost all of them took the opportunity to use the experiment to improve their scientific career.

Almost all doctors were assigned to concentration camps close to their homes or to the universities and research institutes where they were employed. It seems that convenience was the main reason behind the allocation of prisoners to physicians. The Nazi doctors seized the opportunity of using prisoners for their research. Now they had the unique opportunity to conduct research on humans on a massive scale that had been impossible in earlier years.

CHAPTER II

HUMAN EXPERIMENTS IN GERMAN CONCENTRATION CAMPS

The war against the Soviet Union prompted the large-scale human experiments in German concentration camps for two reasons. Firstly, the war in the East demanded solutions to war injuries and epidemics, and military leaders feared biological and chemical warfare. It changed the perspective on German science because only research that contributed to German warfare could count on financial support, material, and ultimately research subjects.

Secondly, the initiatives that led to programs of large-scale human experiments should also be seen about the implementation of the Holocaust. It is generally accepted in the current historiography that the destruction of Jews became an official Nazi policy in the autumn of 1941.

From that moment on, Nazi authorities could use the bodies of Jews for any purpose and without any limits. This genocidal mindset contributed to an overall devaluation of the individual life of all racially inferior people, as they became victims of the Nazi genocidal policies.

Already before the war, concentration camps had, on a small scale, been used for human experiments. Historians differentiate four phases in human experimentation in the Third Reich. The first phase, from 1939 until 1941, took place mainly in clinics and was connected to the Nazi euthanasia program. The coercive experimentation in this phase focused on neurological research. The last three phases took place in the concentration camps.

Between 1939 and 1944 anthropologists and psychologists investigated Jews and Sinti and Roma. The researchers used these groups for sterilization and reproduction experiments. The third phase took place between 1941 and 1943, as a consequence of the war. The experiments dealt with the healing of wounds, infectious diseases, and aviation medicine. Scientists and camp physicians used children as research subjects during the last phase, from 1944 until 1945. The mobilization disrupted the human experiments during the years 1940-1941, when only a few experiments were running.

The experiments can be classified into multiple categories: military surgery, prevention and treatment of epidemics, experiments in the context of aviation medicine, genetic research, and biochemical warfare.

Various organizations and institutes commissioned experiments on humans, such as the SS and the several departments of the Wehrmacht. Individual doctors also seized the opportunity to research humans that had not been possible on this scale in earlier years.

The polycracy of the Third Reich is crucial to understanding the human experiments. The competition and power struggle between various organizations and institutes initiated human experiments: finding solutions to war-related medical issues could give the initiating party more prestige, but more importantly, by acquiring money and facilities for research projects, they could enhance their own position within the Third Reich. Two major organizations commissioned human experiments, the SS and the Wehrmacht. Various institutes and departments within these organizations ordered the experiments. A crucial distinction between the Wehrmacht and the SS intensified their competition. The Wehrmacht had the most prominent and best-educated professors and researchers at its disposal, and the most research projects at affiliated universities and academic institutes. In contrast, the SS lacked qualified medical scientists. However, it had concentration camp inmates as research subjects at its disposal.

The SS was in charge of the concentration camps and the prisoners, and every human experiment needed Himmler's personal permission.

This gave the SS a powerful position about the Wehrmacht.

As Reichsführer-SS, Himmler was in charge of the concentration camps and therefore, he had to permit every human experiment. Himmler had a broad interest in science and alternative medicine. Furthermore, medicine was an important issue to the SS. From the 1930s onwards, the SS developed its own medical division to be independent from the military (Wehrmacht) and civil medicine, as well as to support the establishment of a racially 'pure' society. SS physicians were trained in university clinics and received special training on ideology, racial issues, and eugenics in the medical academy of the SS.

Himmler, together with the historian Hermann Wirth and Walter Darré founded *Ahnenerbe* (ancestral heritage) in 1935. It was an SS appendage devoted to the task of promoting the racial doctrines espoused by Adolf Hitler and his governing Nazi Party, specifically by supporting the idea that the modern Germans descended from an ancient Aryan race seen as biologically superior to other racial groups.

The Wehrmacht depended on Himmler's permission to conduct human experiments. The Wehrmacht had to send research proposals requesting the use of prisoners as guinea pigs to him. Faced with the medical issues of the war, the medical and sanitary services of the Wehrmacht needed to come up with solutions. Because the

Wehrmacht needed Himmler's permission to conduct human experiments in concentration camps it had to act under the tutelage of the SS.

With Himmler's permission, the Wehrmacht ordered human experiments in which their own medical specialists cooperated with the SS.

To understand the behavior of Nazi doctors at the experiments it is crucial to look at the structures behind the experiments. The issue is whether the experiments were initiated from the top down by leading Nazis or whether individual doctors seized the opportunity to benefit from the genocidal conditions.

The majority of the experiments were clearly organized top-down, either by the SS, Ahnenerbe, or the Wehrmacht.

In contrast to the other doctors, Mengele could select his research subjects himself. From the moment he arrived in Auschwitz-Birkenau, he participated in the selection of arriving prisoners and the gassings. He received a promotion after combating a typhus epidemic in a section of the camp by liquidating all prisoners in the barracks. Shortly after his arrival, he started to execute medical experiments.

Although the experiments had a blueprint made by the authorities or the doctors themselves, once the experiments had started, the doctors had much autonomy. Besides carrying out orders, they started to act on their own initiative, using more prisoners in the experiments or arranging personal benefits. The doctors who executed the medical experiments were not under the authority or command of the other doctors employed at the camps, such as the chief camp physician and the camp physician. Overall, they mainly worked directly under the authority of the organizations and institutes that commissioned the experiments.

The Nazi doctors and scientists regarded the concentration camps as a 'vast reservoir of experimental material'.

Once the Nazi doctors had started the experiments, they understood very well the situation they were in and the unlimited possibilities within reach. They came up with new research proposals and demanded new prisoners for their experiments.

Once the Nazi doctors had started to experiment with prisoners, they realized the opportunities that the unlimited availability of research subjects offered to them. They demanded more prisoners, or just took them without approval.

Mengele had the easiest position because he operated in an extermination camp with a vast stream of research subjects doomed to be killed in the gas chambers. Moreover, he could select them himself. He could conduct research that was impossible before, particularly because in Auschwitz many twin pairs were available.

During the experiments, the Nazi doctors held the power over life and death. This was a privilege they did not have under normal circumstances, at least not to this extent. The unlimited power over the lives of their victims influenced their behavior and legitimated their cruel actions towards their victims: in all of this, the man-human background feeling becomes abundantly clear, everything that the happening to victims, makes it seem justified as a matter of course.

The Nazi doctors were keen to use the experiments to improve their scientific careers. This is both true for the old and the young physicians. They realized the unique opportunities the Nazi regime offered them. The younger doctors worked on their Habilitation based on the research from the experiments. The older doctors hoped for a scientific breakthrough. The Nazi doctors were obsessed with exploration. Many physicians were also promoted within the SS based on their execution of the experiments. To put it shortly, from a personal point of view careerism was their prime motivator.

Mengele worked on a Habilitation. Almost all Nazi doctors used expert prisoners as assistants at the experiments. The extensive scale of the experiments asked for extra staff. Particularly the younger physicians were keen to benefit from these experts, and the prisoners had to assist them in writing academic papers. This does not mean these men were pseudo-scientists, they only tried to benefit as much as possible from the opportunities to improve their careers.

In Germany, obtaining a Habilitation is necessary to become a university teacher and in the end a university professor.

For Mengele, who had waited impatiently to distinguish himself and to build an academic career, the twin research in Auschwitz was his momentum. Völklein posed the rhetorical question Mengele must have asked himself: "Up to 350 pairs of twins at the same time that could be questioned, measured and subjected to tests - when and where would such an opportunity again be found for him?" The twin research could bring him academic fame. Moreover, now that the circumstances offered him the opportunity to secure an academic career, Mengele did everything he could to achieve his goal. He conducted many experiments in various fields, most of which he possessed no knowledge on. He used the expertise of his assistants to support him in his research and the writing of academic papers, but he could take the scientific credits himself.

It is clear that the Nazi doctors had a lot to gain by conducting the experiments. The fact whether an experiment was organized top-down or initiated bottom-up did not determine the opportunities the Nazi doctors had. The majority willingly seized the unique opportunity the regime offered them without ethical and moral constraints.

The central question that has puzzled contemporaries and later scientists ever since the public became informed on the human experiments in German concentration camps, is how men and women who have sworn to not harm could deliberately harm and even kill people.

The Nazi doctors kept on experimenting until the final days of the Third Reich. However, when the tide turned against the Third Reich and the collapse became inevitable they started to worry about prosecution. This fear was legitimate because Great Britain, the United States, and the Soviet Union had already in 1943 declared, in a section of the Moscow Declaration, that persons who had committed war crimes and crimes against humanity would be prosecuted after an Allied victory.

In the disturbing final days of the war, the Nazi doctors destroyed as much evidence as possible, but the scale of their crimes made it impossible to prevent the seizure of documents by the Allies. While Allied soldiers liberated Europe from Nazi rule, expert teams followed their trails to collect German research findings to contribute to the Allied warfare. Two fields in particular had their interest, namely nuclear technology and biological and medical military research.

As a side effect of the screenings of German scientists and the investigations, the Allies became informed of the medical crimes committed in concentration camps. Victims of human experiments and former prisoners also brought the atrocities under the attention of the Allies as victim groups started to collect documents in various concentration camps. This contributed to a growing record of legal evidence.

The doctors in concentrations camps at the outskirts of the German sphere of influence, such as Auschwitz, were the first to be confronted with the advancing Allied armies. The Germans abandoned the concentration camps and the physicians had to leave their research stations in a hurry. They knew that their actions had been criminal offenses and that the Allies would hold them accountable for war crimes if they were caught. Therefore, they tried to transport their research material back to Germany and destroy as much remaining evidence as possible.

Hirt and Haagen were the first doctors confronted with the Allied forces when the American army advanced in the direction of Alsace in November 1944. Hirt feared that the Americans would discover his skeleton collection and had already asked Sievers for directions in October. The head of Ahnenerbe submitted the urgent question to Himmler, offering three possible solutions: maintenance of the collection, partial destruction, or complete destruction. Himmler or his assistant Brandt decided that the collection had to be destroyed.

On 23 November 1944, the American army captured Strasbourg. Hirt had already left the city one week earlier, unable to destroy the skeleton collection. The French resistance and the American soldiers discovered the skeleton collection in the cellars of the Anatomical Institute and arrested Hirt's anatomical assistant Dr. Otto Bong.

An Allied journalist published an article on the gruesome topic in the *Daily Mail* on 3 January 1945. Nevertheless, the Allies did not yet know the full scale of the crime.

Hirt's reaction was desperate and exculpatory, arguing that all countries had skeleton collections, including France and the United Kingdom, and that the Germans had found bodies as well at the Anatomical Institute in Strasbourg when they occupied the city in 1940.

Hirt argued that he did not work on racial issues, except for the major anthropological skull collection, consisting of skulls of Germans, English, French, Japanese, Chinese, Negroes, Egyptians, and so on, that already existed in Strasbourg: "It was my self-evident duty to preserve this skull collection and to follow the tradition of the institute possibility to continue from a modern point of view".

The bodies came from criminals convicted to death, though, it was inevitable that during wartime more bodies were available because of epidemics. Hirt claimed he decided to build research facilities at Natzweiler because he had not enough space to hold his guinea pigs at the Anatomical Institute. He placed his devices and instruments at the disposal of the camp physician after he asked for Hirt's support on microscopic research. Hirt executed sections on human bodies twice, which was a common practice around the world, according to him. The accusation that he infected prisoners with various diseases was so ignorant, that it did not need refutation: the nonsense of claiming having vaccinated inmates with a serious disease is probably already led to absurdity by the fact that at most a madman would dare a Camp, in which several thousand people are, with such seriously infectious diseases to contaminate.

Lastly, Hirt claimed ironically that the commission had mistaken the delousing chamber for a gas chamber.

Clauberg and Mengele had to leave their research facilities in Auschwitz in January 1945. Clauberg moved via Gross-Rosen to Ravensbrück, where he continued his sterilization experiments on another 35 women. After the war, he moved to Schleswig-Holstein where Soviet troops arrested him on 8 June 1945.

Mengele also went from Auschwitz to Gross-Rosen. He brought many samples and research files back to Germany but was also forced to destroy many files that could be used as evidence against him. In the final months of the war, he worked in several camps, constantly on the move from the advancing troops. American troops finally arrested him in June 1945. He was well aware of his crimes and tried to avoid prosecution: he wore a Wehrmacht uniform and probably used a false name. The Americans were unaware of his identity, also because of the absence of a SS tattoo on Mengele's body, and he was released after only six weeks. Mengele went immediately into hiding in Mangolding, Upper Bavaria.

The Allies prosecuted the highest functionaries of the Third Reich at the Nuremberg Trial immediately after the war. Nevertheless, they also wanted to prosecute lower ranks of the Nazi hierarchy that committed crimes. The Allied Control Council Law No. 10, issued on 20 December 1945, made their prosecution possible because it authorized every occupying power in Germany to prosecute war criminals in their own national jurisdiction. The following crimes would be prosecuted: crimes against peace, planning and implementing an aggressive war, war crimes, crimes against humanity, and membership of a criminal organization.

While the prosecutors of the United States prepared a trial against the main perpetrators of medical crimes in the Third Reich, they had already brought the first Nazi doctor who had executed human experiments to justice.

The largest trial against perpetrators of medical crimes during the time of the Third Reich was the Nuremberg Medical Trial. The United States founded the American Military Tribunal (AMT) after the Nuremberg Trial, to prosecute high-ranking Nazi officials grouped by their profession.

The United States indicted the accused on four counts. Count One charged the defendants with conspiracy of war crimes and crimes against humanity. Count Two and Count Three were the main counts of the indictment because those counts dealt directly with the human experiments. Count Two charged the accused with war crimes, because the experiments had been executed 'without the subjects' consent, upon civilians and members of the armed forces of nations then at war with the German Reich and who were in the custody of the German Reich in the exercise of belligerent control.'

Count Three declared the human experiments as crimes against humanity.

The Soviet Union also prosecuted Nazi doctors for human experiments. Clauberg and Kremer, who had both committed their crimes in Auschwitz, were prosecuted in the Soviet Union. British soldicrs arrested Kremer for his SS membership in August 1945. During his imprisonment in Neuengamme, the Allies discovered his diary and became aware of his involvement in Auschwitz crimes. They extradited him to Poland at the end of 1946. The Polish Supreme People's Tribunal in Cracow sentenced him to death on 22 December 1947, but within one month, the sentence was repealed to life imprisonment. Kremer was released from prison in 1958 because of good behavior, his old age, and illness. He returned to Münster, where the German authorities arrested him.

The Russians transported Clauberg after his arrest to Moscow, where he was sentenced to twenty-five years imprisonment in 1948. However, the court convicted him for the mass murder of political prisoners and not for the experiments.

The Soviet Union gave him amnesty in 1955. Back in the German Federal Republic, the authorities arrested him again. He died during his trial in 1957 because of a stroke.

Clauberg and Kremer faced the longest judicial consequences for their participation in the human experiments.

Mengele escaped his imminent prosecution. Mengele also fled to South-America. He remained in hiding in Mangolding and escaped via Italy to Argentina in 1949. Because he was never brought to justice, he could become a mythical figure. Comparing Mengele with Eichmann: the former remained a symbol of evil, the latter was 'again reduced to "normal human proportions"' during his trial in Jerusalem in 1962.

The Nazi doctors gave various arguments to legitimate the execution of human experiments during the trials. Some of these arguments were plausible, however, most of them were mere retrospective justifications to exonerate themselves from their crimes. The justifications concerned extraordinary circumstances, the research subjects, and their own involvement.

First, the Nazi doctors argued that various extraordinary circumstances made human experiments necessary and unavoidable. The argument of warfare made sense to a certain extent because it was part of the National Socialist mindset during the war. The Third Reich demanded that everybody contributed to German warfare. The National Socialist argument was that if soldiers placed their lives at risk at the front, the prisoners at concentration camps should also sacrifice their lives.

However, there is no proof that the human experiments made a significant difference to the warfare, neither to the soldiers at the front nor to the citizens at the home front.

Despite the absence of direct results of the human experiments, the Nazi doctors emphasized the scientific value of the experiments to the court. The defendants also argued that time pressure made it impossible to develop a detailed research design including animal experiments and the use of volunteers as research subjects. All of the defendants argued that they would not have executed the experiment under normal, peacetime circumstances. The claim made by the Nazi doctors of the imminent dangers and threats because of the war is a legitimate argument in the sense that at the time they really believed the experiments could benefit German warfare. Nevertheless, as is the case with all their exonerating arguments, this does not legitimize the experiments on humans, legally nor morally.

The rhetorical question the Nazi doctors asked themselves was whether it was legitimate to sacrifice a small group of people to save the lives of tens of thousands of soldiers. According to them, it was reasonable to sacrifice a small minority for the benefits of the majority, or even, for the sake of humanity.

The Nazi doctors tried to exonerate themselves by claiming that many countries executed human experiments on prisoners, including the United States, and that there were no universal legal and ethical guidelines for human experimentation. Without precise and written guidelines, they could not have violated ethical standards. Following the legal principle of *nullum crimen sine lege scripta, certa praevia* (no crime without prior written, certain, law) they had not even committed a crime and could not be held legally accountable. However, the prosecution at the Nuremberg Trial could easily demonstrate that the Nazi doctors had violated their own laws, namely the guidelines of 1931 that obligated informed and voluntary consent for human experiments.

The defendants also legitimized the use of concentration camp prisoners. All of them claimed they only had used persons convicted to death. They argued that it was legitimate to use the prisoners because their death was inevitable.

The defendants supported the claim of voluntary participation with the argument that the prisoners benefitted from their participation in the experiment. The prisoners received nutritious food, became immune to various diseases, were saved from inevitable execution or death, and afterward would be pardoned by the regime.

The argument that the prisoners benefitted from their participation is obviously false. In some cases, the research subjects received more food, but only to improve their health to match the physical condition of German soldiers, and only as long as the experiment lasted. The immunization argument does not need refutation because the doctors infected the prisoners with diseases without their consent. Moreover, many prisoners died because of these diseases. The Nazi doctors did not care for the life of the prisoners. More importantly, never was a prisoner released for his or her participation in experiments.

Besides the legitimations concerning the situational factors and the victims, the Nazi doctors also defended their own role in the experiments. The defendants used the common defense strategy of the *Befehlsnotstand:* they acted under orders and could not refuse to execute them. They argued that just like soldiers at the front, they had to fulfill their duty and obey every order.

When the horrible crimes of the Nazi doctors were discussed at the Nuremberg Medical Trial, the cry for universal rules for human experiments became imminent. Never again should people be forced to place their bodies at the disposal of individuals, states, and science. The Nuremberg Code, which provided universal guidelines for human experimentation, emerged out of this dark period in history.

CHAPTER III

MENGELE'S BACKGROUND AND AUSCHWITZ YEARS

Without question, the Third Reich"s unique export of genocide is the most influential characteristic of the twentieth century. In total, upwards of twenty-one million souls were murdered during the Nazi reign either in concentration camps or by mobilized killing squads such as the Einsatzgruppen. A primary component of the Holocaust was the research conducted by Nazi physicians on uninformed and unsuspecting prisoners.

Educated and trained to aid and ensure the quality of life, the physicians collaborated with the Third Reich to create unfathomable feats of torture and murder in the name of science. Adolf Hitler"s shining beacon of the Final Solution, the Auschwitz concentration camp, was called home by possibly the most infamous Nazi physician. Josef Mengele worked tirelessly in Auschwitz to unlock the programmability of human genetics by experimenting on young children. This book will detail Mengele"s research and deconstruct the changing medical and deontological ethical landscape which promulgated the environment of government-supported human torture.

Josef Mengele"s upbringing in the small Bavarian hamlet of Gunzburg, Germany was aristocratic, albeit nothing spectacular. His family prospered financially due to the machinery factory founded by his father, Karl, and operated by the stern matriarch. Josef, unlike his brothers, was wholly disinterested in learning the family trade. Instead, he dreamed of distinction in scientific academia. At a young age, Josef struggled with his marks in grade school, earning only average grades, certainly nothing inspiring that foretold his future academic achievements. Mengele instead spent his formative years parading around town with his brothers in the most fashionable outfits, cavorting with the young local girls at cafes and theatres. He often effused to his schoolmates that the Mengele name would be heard on the radio and all would be proud to know him. Josef Mengele was only partially correct in his prediction, for his enthusiastic drive for achievement ultimately led him to commit the most heinous of atrocities on the most innocent of victims.

Early in his education, Mengele chose courses in anatomy and science, hoping to further his career in a broad medical research field rather than confining himself to a specific discipline. He opted instead for medicine with an emphasis on "anthropology and human genetics, so he could study the whole range of medicine. Zealous industriousness enabled Mengele to earn doctorates in Anthropology from Munich University and in medicine from Frankfurt University. During this period Mengele did not advertise virulent anti-Semitism, though he was already a rising member of the Nazi Party. While his original doctoral thesis focused on the jaw structure and the construction of four separate racial groups, there is nothing present that articulates racial motivations. Mengele"s two theses, accepted by each university, were panned as rather dry and uninspiring.

Simultaneously, more important political storms were brewing in Germany. Years before, in Gunzburg, Mengele had joined the Nazi Party but only seemed moderately interested in their politics. As he advanced professionally in Munich, the racial hygienic aspect of the Nazi platform became increasingly attractive. It is difficult to pinpoint a definitive date at which Mengele became fully engrossed in Nazi racial propaganda. However, his immersion may be a result of the political climate and that his real interest in genetics and evolution happened to coincide with the developing concept that some human beings afflicted by disorders were unfit to reproduce, even to live. Josef

Mengele“s scientific aspirations soon became influenced by specific ideologies and professional mentors that would shape the research of Cell Block 10 in the Auschwitz concentration camp.

The most influential figure in Mengele“s early career was Otmar Freiherr von Verschuer, considered the most respected racial hygienist in Germany. It was von Verschuer who pushed Mengele into the study of twin genetics. Under von Verschuer's aegis, Mengele learned that it was acceptable – even desirable – to experiment on human beings if it advanced a scientific cause. Moreover, von Verschuer imparted to Mengele the necessity of using innumerable experimental subjects. Josef“s dedication and tutelage would ideally result in tenure with the highest German universities, notoriety which Mengele seriously craved.

A primary legislative influence on the young doctor was the enactment of the Law for the Protection of Hereditary Health. This extreme governmental measure detailed the sterilization qualifications for several groups categorized as subhuman. Chief among those groups were schizophrenics, manic depressives, alcoholics, the blind, any individual suffering physical deformities, and homosexuals, among others. This legislation gave Mengele the political impetus to operate free from prosecution. He was now fully engrossed with the Nazi cause of racial hygienics. He was convinced he served a great cause, an attempt by Hitler to prevent mankind from self-destructing. He became the incarnation of Nazism in its extreme. Several mitigating factors, from the centuries-old European seedling of anti-Semitism to the experimental freedom Nazism provided, from the influence of von Verschuer to the changing political landscape resulted in a potent recipe for mass murder.

Mengele"s reputation grew quickly through the upper echelon of the Nazi government, and he was soon charged by Heinrich Himmler to craft a directive for the occupied territories of the lebensraum. Mengele succeeded in working with Himmler on an extensive four-point plan:

I. The annexed territories were to be thoroughly cleansed of non-Germans;
II. persons claiming any German blood would be classified according to documentary evidence first, and lacking that, by racial examination; those in doubtful categories as well as "renegade" {anti-Nazi or "Polish minded"}
III. Germans would be segregated and subjected to special conditions to ensure "re-education and good behavior persons exhibiting Germanic features would also undergo racial examinations to determine if their ancestors had been "Polanized"; positive cases would be removed from Poland for better re-Germanization in the Reich proper;
IV. similar procedures would be carried out upon orphans from Polish orphanages as well as children coming under public care.

It is the section under „racial examinations" that Mengele contributed the most expertise. Through his work with Himmler, Mengele procured the legality of extensively studying each minute anatomical characteristic with the understanding that doctors could decipher any undesirable ancestral blood by simple physical examination. That diagnosis would forever change the life of the patient as imprisonment, exile, or death was oftentimes the result.

Furthermore, in 1933, the Law for the Prevention of Progeny With Hereditary Disease was ratified. This piece of legislation further skewed the reality about legalizing unethical behavior. It is from this frame of reference that the concept of "special treatment" must be approached... These efforts on behalf of "national health" and the "integrity of the German people" can thus be classified under three main headings:

1. The euthanasia program for the "incurably sick."
2. The direct extermination, using "special treatment," of racial groups and patients considered undesirable.
3. Preliminary experimental work in mass sterilization.

This proclamation, combined with the overall provisions established in the Law for the Protection of Hereditary Health, provided Mengele with the opportunity to accumulate disposable experimental subjects. For the next decade, Mengele grew more emboldened and became more willing to take science past the levels of acceptability. World War II soon erupted, and Mengele accepted an appointment to the elite medical division of the Waffen SS. Early in his deployment with the SS, he was awarded two medals: the Black Badge for the Wounded and the Medal for the Care of the German People. Under heavy fire, Mengele had administered aid to two fellow soldiers and was instrumental in saving their lives. These medals were proudly displayed by Mengele in the following years, even while administering selection at the Auschwitz death camp.

Josef Mengele would emerge as the medical symbol of the Nazi concentration camps. His stoic nature and high military fashion became the enduring illustration of the macabre selections at Auschwitz. Josef Mengele had become the incarnation of its monstrosity – cool, detached, and always immaculately prepared for the long-drawn-out rituals of death... With the simple wave of his gloved hand, Mengele appropriated hundreds of thousands of men, women, and children immediately to the gas chambers. Those poor souls, unfortunately, were lucky. For it was the children, and most especially twins, which caught Mengele"s eye. Nazi medicinal dogma mandated that the Aryan race could be categorically bread to perfection. By doing so, the German state could reproduce at an astounding rate, thereby populating their rightful lands and defeating the treachery of Jews, Gypsies, homosexuals, and other undesirables.

To achieve this utopia, Mengele would have to unlock the programmability of human reproduction. For many years he was lacking what he envisioned as the ideal situation, namely unlimited human experimentation. However, through the cavalcade of political evolutions and societal acceptability, Mengele would soon enjoy the freedom of experimentation and responsibility that only the Auschwitz concentration camp could offer. By standing guard at the selection ramps, Mengele was able to personally select his human test subjects each day. He often proclaimed his astonishment at both the number of available subjects and the remarkable power he held over the prisoners.

Mengele"s primary aim in research was to prove that certain traits were inherited and thusly could be bred out of existence. Included in these traits were eye color, obesity, and certain nasal features. The ultimate goal was to produce an ideal race of Aryan men and women endowed with only the finest genetic traits, who would rapidly multiply and rule the world. This potential medical breakthrough and the manipulation of traits through careful breeding practices would make Mengele universally famous.

Mengele understood he could only achieve professional success through industrious determination, for he knew he was not as gifted as his contemporaries. He held that "if he only worked hard enough, performed enough experimental studies, tested a sufficient number of twins, then he would be recognized as the great scientist he thought he was". It may even be that Mengele"s monstrous experiments were the physical manifestation of subconscious feelings of ineptitude. Primary among these being that von Verschuer was the racial hygienist mastermind. It was von Verschuer who was admitted to the American Eugenics Society, not Mengele. It was von Verschuer who stayed out of the desolate concentration camps and worked at the Kaiser Wilhelm Institute (later renamed the Max Planck Institute) while Mengele was forced to be away from his wife and newborn son.

But despite his dedication and fanaticism, the mediocre student of Gunzburg never possessed any real brilliance. The tests, questionnaires, and many of the experiments themselves appear to have been the brainchild of Verschuer. Mengele“s reality did not match his delusions. He was only the lackey of von Verschuer, not the medical genius he had hoped.

Undaunted, Mengele strove to out-research his more respected contemporaries. Auschwitz experiments were seen by Mengele as being crucial in achieving his personal goal of an academic career. They were to be used as part of his "habilitation," which was required for university appointments. He began to push the ethical boundaries of his profession and experienced no professional backlash. The outcome was so-called legalized human experimentation and unchecked torture conducted solely for personal gain.

The litany of crimes committed by Mengele at Auschwitz is astonishing. It is humanly incomprehensible that the institutionalized torture and murder of children occurred in plain view at Cell Block 10. Mengele was transfixed by the uniqueness of the twins in Auschwitz, and he finally supervised his own laboratory, free from the direct supervision of von Verschuer. Even though Dr. Eduard Wirths was stationed as the Chief SS doctor at Auschwitz, Mengele“s power was never monitored or questioned. Mengele began to experiment with children immediately after placement in the small Polish town of Oswiecim.

Children, strapped to slabs of marble, had their spines, eyes, and inner organs probed, injected, and cut, often with unknown chemicals and without anesthetic. However, Mengele"s experiments were incomplete. While Auschwitz provided Mengele with identical twins and the opportunity to use one as the control in his experiments, he has not presented a detailed medical history of each patient, thereby rendering his experiments baseless. Each individual brought to the Auschwitz gate was not required to bring their medical history; therefore Mengele could not discern which characteristic was genetic and which was environmental. This incomplete knowledge would have been understood by a professional such as Mengele, unfortunately, it did not seem to sufficiently matter. Furthermore, Nazi political pressure pushed Mengele to increase his number of experiments. This was especially interesting to the Nazi regime, in particular about a desired increase in the birth rate through a medically manipulated increase in the number of births of twins. One trait Mengele researched is the occurrence of twins having different colored eye pigmentation. Subsequently, Mengele began to experiment with the eye pigmentation in an attempt to discover the cause for the difference or, conversely, to determine if he could alter the pigmentation.

Thirty-six children from one barrack in Birkenau were used for the eye tests, which resulted in painful infections and sometimes blindness. After the tests, the children served no further use, and so they were gassed. After gassing the eyes were removed and shipped back to the Kaiser Wilhelm Institute, presumably to von Verschuer. In Auschwitz, this pattern of experimentation then gassing became typical under Mengele. Once a child was judged as unnecessary or the experiments were complete, that child was murdered.

Following selection, a child would be brought to a special camp section which solely housed Mengele"s specimens. These young prisoners were given better shelter, healthcare, and food than the other Auschwitz residents for the purpose that Mengeleneeded the children in enhanced health for his experiments. It must have been surreal to watch Mengele interact with the children. Moments after motioning the rest of a child's family to the gas chambers, he would dote on the young orphan and ensure that any needs were accommodated. "Uncle Mengele," as they called him, delighted them with candy, joked with them, hugged and kissed them. There exist camp survivor stories of present-day adults fondly remembering this aspect of imprisonment. While the torture and medical practices were barbaric, Mengele routinely treated the children better than most SS officers.

Moreover, Mengele was violently protective of his children and presided over upwards of six hundred prisoners at one time. The camp had a special wing, B2F, from which Mengele conducted his "in vivo" experiments; that is, experiments conducted while the children were alive, oftentimes without anesthetics. In many cases, typhus and tuberculosis were injected into one "healthy" twin to see how each reacted to the disease. Once again, the moment the study was completed, the children were murdered.

Several times Mengele rushed to save his subjects from a premature death at the hands of the gas chambers. "At one point towards the end of the war, I was scheduled to go to the chambers... that"s when I saw Mengele. We were taken off the truck. He stopped the whole procession because they were going to kill his twins." In the same People Magazine article Rene"s sister, Irene, recalls the selection ramp with Mengele, impeccably dressed, repeatedly bellowing out for twins. Dr. Martina Puzyna, a prisoner doctor, recollects on the time she witnessed Mengele running alongside a cattle car of Hungarian Jews screaming for twins to emerge. Dr. Puzyna remembers Mengele"... shrieking in a loud voice..." and acting quite maniacally. He exhibited unimaginable fury at the prospect of missing out on more research subjects.

Once chosen by Mengele, the children were taken to the hospital, cleaned, deloused, and intensely examined. One of Mengele's captive doctors, Martina Puzyna, was responsible for these examinations. Each measurement was painstakingly noted, and Puzyna often worked to delay the processing, for once the measurements were complete the children were available to Mengele.

A witness, Vera Alexander, described one of Mengele“s experiments:

> *One day Mengele brought chocolate and special clothes. The next day, SS men came and took two children away. They were two of my pets, Tito and Nino. One of them was a hunchback. Two or three days later, an SS man brought them back in a terrible state. They had been cut. The hunchback was sewn to the other child, back to back, their wrists back to back too. There was a terrible smell of gangrene. The cuts were dirty and the children cried every night.*

Alexander went on to describe blood transfusions between twins so that Mengele could observe each child“s reaction. Oftentimes the children endured high fevers and terrible headaches and if the child cried too often as a result of the pain, he or she was gassed. Mengele worked tirelessly to ensure his test subjects died at precisely the same time. This would ensure the internal reaction to any stimulus could be accurately documented.

Following Germany“s defeat in 1945, a West German Indictment listed Mengeleamongst its criminals. The indictment alleges as follows:

> *... Mengele had 100 children shot in the back of the head for his autopsies. Heis also said to have lured some of the more unwilling children to the crematorium from the experimental block by offering them sweets and then shooting them on the*

way. One of his most common methods of ensuring simultaneous deaths was to inject chloroform into their hearts, coagulating the blood and causing heart failure.

Mengele soon ordered the construction of an updated research and pathology division to better conduct autopsies. Mengele acted in explicitly destructive ways to newborns and their mothers."He is said to have stood on pregnant women"s stomachs until the fetuses were expelled; he is even said to have dissected a one-year-old while the child was still alive." Mengele ordered mothers to cover their breasts with tape and they were prohibited from nourishing the child. In several cases, sympathetic nurses smuggled morphine from the hospital so the mothers could mercy-kill the child. Furthermore, Mengele is "...said to have thrown a newborn baby onto a stove, angered at the mother's pregnancy which the selection doctors had failed to spot and which would have normally qualified her for the gas chamber..." Due to the lack of decent medical facilities available to the prisoners, Josef Mengele ordered all pregnant women to be immediately gassed.

Many times, children Mengele deemed unworthy for his most important experimentation received immediate and terrible deaths. A survivor, Annani SilovichPet'ko, gave a sworn statement to the following:

After a while, a large group of SS officers arrived on motorcycles, Mengeleamong them. They drove into the yard and got off their motorcycles. Upon arriving they circled the flames; it burned horizontally. We watched to see what would follow. After a while trucks arrived, dump trucks, with children inside. There were about ten of these trucks. After they had entered the yard an officer gave an order and the trucks backed up to the fire and they started throwing those children right into the fire, into the pit. The children started to scream;

some of them managed to crawl out of the burning pit; an officer walked around it with sticks and pushed back those who managed to get out. Hoess and Mengele were present and were giving orde... They were all under five years old.

Mengele"s insatiable need to experiment continued to escalate. It is estimated that only a hundred or so set of twins survived Auschwitz out of the nearly three thousand that entered. So obsessed was he with finding vast numbers of twins that he attended railhead selections even when it was not his turn; he could be seen bargaining with the SS physicians on duty to set the twins aside for him. While many of the other SS doctors turned to alcohol to cope with their regular duties of railhead selection, Mengelebartered for more opportunities. He often dressed in his Waffen-SS best and stood sentry for hours.

An important voice to the medical horrors of Auschwitz comes from MiklosNyiszli. The Jewish Hungarian doctor was transported to Auschwitz with his wife and daughter in 1944 and soon became employed as Mengele"s personal pathologist. Immediately following the war, Nyiszli published a detailed account of what he witnessed as part of the Jewish *sonderkommando*. He begins by explaining the benefits of experimenting in a concentration camp:

The confines of the KZ [Auschwitz Concentration Camp] offered vast possibilities for research, first in the field of forensic medicine, because of the high suicide rate, and also in the field of pathology, because of the relatively high percentage of dwarfs, giants, and other abnormal types of human beings. The abundance – unequaled elsewhere in the world – of corpses, and the fact that one could dispose of them freely for purposes of research, opened wider horizons.

Nyiszli reaffirms the fact that, concerning scientific experimentation, the need for fresh corpses to autopsy was paramount. The uniqueness of having so many twins living in a centralized location was especially appealing to the Nazis, for it presented a capacity for research unavailable throughout human history.

Unfortunately, to detail precisely how one twin reacted to an injection or stimulus, both specimens had to die at precisely the same time. Nyiszli details his horror at discovering this practice:

> *I began the dissection of one set of twins and recorded each phase of my work... In the exterior coat of the left ventricle was a small red spot caused by a hypodermic injection... There could be no mistake... Normally the blood contained in the left ventricle is taken out and weighed. This method could not be employed in the present case, because the blood was coagulated into a compact mass. I extracted the coagulum with the forceps and brought it to my nose. I was struck by the characteristic odor of chloroform. The victim had received an injection of chloroform to the heart... and cause instantaneous death by heart failure... Not only did they [Third Reich] kill with gas, but also with injections of chloroform into the heart.*

Nyiszli further notes that Mengele had spoken with the pathologist following his gruesome discovery. As you can see, Mengele remarked, these children suffered from syphilis and would have suffered a slow and gruesome death. The Third Reich did not have the medical capacity to prevent their suffering, and therefore, Mengele was quietly saving the children from further pain.

The absurdity with which Mengele performed his experiments is infinite. He would order twin sisters to have pre-pubescent sex with other twin boys to determine if this would provide a higher rate of twin babies. "When we objected that such an experiment was impermissible he told us that we were prisoners and that we had no say in the matter." Mengele soon began a routine of shooting or ordering the gassing of any patient who dissented.

The appearance of Mengele"s personality "doubling" was often on full display. It manifested itself in how he treated the children first and foremost, but most especially how he treated pregnant women. Mengele was seen treating a pregnant inmate through the labor process; especially taking "...all correct medical precautions during childbirth, rigorously observing all aseptic principles, cutting the umbilical cord with the greatest care, etc." No more than thirty minutes later, Mengele dispatched the mother and newborn to be gassed. In this case, the two sides of Mengele, the beneficent doctor and the murderer, were both present. Mengele"s physician side eased the labor suffering of the mother, and when that task was complete, the Auschwitz Mengele reemerged, immediately marking the woman and newborn for death.

Moreover, Mengele was instrumental in resolving unique problems with the extermination process. Mengele once witnessed a bottleneck at the crematorium, which was rendering the gassing process inefficient. The Nazi doctor resolved the issue by ordering trenches to be dug and filled with gasoline. Both the dead and the living, adults as well as children and infants, were thrown bodily into these pits to be destroyed under Mengele"s supervision. This resolved the immediate issue of the bottleneck, and the gassing soon resumed acceptable levels of efficiency.

Marc Berkowitz and his sister Francesca were brought to Auschwitz from Czechoslovakia with their parents in early 1944. Marc and Francesca were quickly selected by Mengele for experimentation. "They put us in freezing baths, smeared chemicals on our skin, but it was the needles we were most afraid of. After the first 150 injections, I stopped counting..." Berkowitz even witnessed his mother marching toward the gas chamber, after which Mengele mocked the child by asking if he still believed in God.

Moshe Offer is a survivor of Mengele"s experiments. He witnessed the slow murder of his brother, Tibi, while in Auschwitz. "One surgery on his spine left my brother paralyzed. He could not walk anymore. Then they took out his sexual organs. After the fourth operation, I did not see Tibi anymore." Auschwitz had taken Offer'smother, father, and two older brothers at the selection ramp, and now Moshe witnessed the slow murder of his only remaining relative at the hands of Josef Mengele. Mengele's experiments lacked any sense of professionalism, and his dissections were oftentimes stodgy and ill-prepared. An Aryan-looking Jew from Poland, Josef Rosenblum, came to Auschwitz and worked his way as a slave employee intoMengele's care. Unbeknownst to his guards, Rosenblum understood German. As a result, Rosenblum was able to document many conversations Mengele had with his staff in the hospital.

First and foremost, Rosenblum tells of the sloppiness with which the experiments were conducted. "It autopsy indeed was a mess. All the corpses had been cut into bloody pieces. There were piles of body parts on the wooden tables, which were about twelve feet long and four feet wide, peppered with numerous bloodstained nicks."

However, there was a side to Mengele, the other side of his "doubling", which saved Rosenblum from certain death. For several months Rosenblumhad worked tirelessly to clean Mengele's office, the offices of his subordinate physicians, and even polished Mengele's boots once a day. This was done strictly out of self-preservation, and it ultimately proved helpful. Rosenblum developed an infection behind his Mastoid bone, which nearly killed the young Pole. Joe was operated on by

Mengele and even given anesthetics. The surgery was arranged by a fellow inmate called only "Father," and done because Mengele wished to reward Joe for his diligence in cleaning the office. Following the surgery, Rosenblum was permitted to recuperate in the hospital, an honor never before bestowed upon a Jewish prisoner. Joe was provided warm farina, buttered bread, and milk for the several days of his recovery.

Once or twice a day, Mengele would stop by Rosenblum's bed and inquire as to how his incision was healing. After a week or two, Rosenblum was simply allowed to pack up his new clothes, given to him by the hospital staff, and walk out of the front door back into the main camp. Rosenblum directly attributes his camp survival to the operation and care Mengele provided.

Meanwhile, Mengele would return to the selection platform, the location where he spent a vast majority of his free time. Mengele would dress himself in his military best, no matter the weather, and separate the incoming prisoners for hours on end.

As the German war effort devolved and more German men and boys were being recruited into the fighting forces, the need for slave labor increased. During the earlier selections, Mengele routinely gassed mothers with their children. Now, however, Mengele began sending the mothers to the work camps. Rosenblum notes that, following this separation, the children were still executed. The behavior change was not a noble gesture; Mengele was still ordering the murder of innocent children. Only now, the mothers were kept alive, knowing full well the fate of their offspring. On one unique day, Rosenblum overheard Mengele discussing the war with several of his subordinates. While cleaning the office, Rosenblum took notes when the discussion turned to the justifications behind the genocide. Unlike most Nazis, Mengeleseemed to function without any overriding sense of anti-Semitism. Rather, he authorized the gassing of Jewish prisoners on a more philosophical level. "Actually, we never had anything against the Jewish people... Hitler wanted to be smarter than the rest of the world, so we had to eliminate the Jews... they never did anything to us."

Mengele went on to exclaim that the Jews were highly successful in business, science, and the arts. The Aryan race desired supremacy among all human endeavors and therefore the Jewish population could not continue. The world could not support the coexistence of two master races. Summarily, the Aryan leadership had decided to eradicate the Jews from civilization. To see such a startling acknowledgment from Mengele is chilling, as it adds another layer to his rationalization for the Auschwitzexperiments. Mengele was, by most accounts, actively murdering innocent children to advance his career in post-war Germany.

After Auschwitz was liberated, Mengele escaped prosecution with the help of Nazi sympathizers and settled in South America. A reasonable query is if Mengele was, indeed, remorseful for his behavior. His son, Rolf, who had only briefly met Mengelewhen he was very young, traveled to South America to confront his father and ask that very pointed question. Mengele remarked as follows:

> *...his job was to clarify only "able to work" and "unable to work". He graded people as "able to work" as often as possible. He thinks he saved the lives of several thousand people that way. He didn't order the extermination and he was not responsible. He said the twins owe their lives to him. He said he never harmed anybody personally, and he got very excited at this point.*

Rolf departed the bungalow with a vibrant disgust for his father and what he had committed. Josef Mengele, the butcher of children at Auschwitz, had somehow turned himself into a victim.

The town of Candido Godoi, Brazil is often cited as the prime example of Mengelecontinuing his experimentation into twin reproduction. There are reports of a higher concentration of twin births in this town, and it is fact that Mengele visited there several times while in hiding. However, to associate Mengele as being instrumental in CandidoGodoi"s high twin birth rate is misleading. There are two main points of contention:

1. It turns out that Cândido Godói experienced no notable change in the twin birthrate in the 1960s. According to the town's baptismal records, twins had been unusually common in the town since at least the 1920s, decades beforeMengele's arrival. Twin births are still common in the town today, decades after Mengele's death. Even if Mengele had developed some ovulation induction drug, it would have affected only that generation; he had no knowledge or ability to modify genetic code, which would have been necessary to pass the trait to future generations.
2. Cândido Godói's twin rate is very high, but not extraordinarily high compared to similar towns in the region. It turns out that many such communities, not only inSouth America but worldwide, consisting of small, isolated populations, often expatriates, have high twin rates. In particular, isolated villages in Nigeria and Romania have similar histories and similar twin rates.

While Mengele did spend time in Candido Godoi, there is no evidence to prove that he conducted any experimentation in the town. While in South America, Mengeleposed as a farmworker, a veterinarian, and worked many menial jobs. However, he never practiced medicine on humans again, aside from allegedly treating MartinBormann“s stomach cancer and performing the occasional illegal abortion. Josef Mengele conducted experiments on an untold number of children at the Auschwitz concentration camp. His research caused the mutilation and murder of a high percentage of its young prisoners, and Mengele successfully evaded prosecution for his crimes, ultimately drowning in a Brazilian lake in 1979.

What remains behind is a catalog of scientific data for future generations to assess. The quest then becomes to determine which factors changed in Germany that allowed for Mengele's experiments. While documenting the horrific tales of children in the Auschwitz concentration camp, it is important to note that Josef Mengele committed no crime due to the specific nature of German law. The morphing political, professional, and deontological ethics within Germany created an environment that allowed for the acceptability of Mengele“s torture of children.

CHAPTER IV

MENGELE'S PROFESSIONAL ETHICS

German society of the early twentieth century was considered enlightened and civilized. Yet in this educated society the systematic extermination of millions was enabled, and chief among these facilitators was the medical profession. Close analysis of the German medical ideal of Lebenswelten Lebens', or life unworthy of life, allows a picture to form as to how the medical community encouraged the establishment of camps such as Auschwitz.

The total number of men, women, and children murdered by the Third Reich was not strictly limited to European Jews. The entire figure more likely approached — ...21 million men, women, handicapped, aged, sick, prisoners of war, forced laborers, camp inmates, critics, homosexuals, Jews, Slavs, Serbs, Czechs, Italians, Poles, Frenchmen, Ukrainians, and so on. It is estimated that this number includes roughly one million children. The true number could easily be higher, and this killing environment emerged through the collaboration of doctors and legislators. The evolving ethics of the German medical profession led to a frigid environment where the life of the patient no longer mattered.

Before Josef Mengele was authorized to experiment, he was obligated to submit a classification report detailing his study and categorizing the nature of each trial. The two classifications were state-sponsored and educational research. The state-sponsored category was well regulated and quite limiting in its scope. The second, and more dangerous, did not have the same structures and parameters as the state-sponsored experiment. Even though the state-sponsored research carried with it a strict set of guidelines, Mengele was not confined to its regulations.

Mengele's research fell within the educational parameters, and therefore he did not have to present any findings to an oversight board. As a fellow doctor in Auschwitz would later write, Mengele's method — ...was descriptive, the amassing of data, and I know of no evidence that he had any significantly original scientific ideas. Mengele marked his research as educational by arguing that the data-generating would be useful to future researchers. Therefore, any non-scientific research was not identified and prohibited. As a result, the only superior he was responsible to was von Verschuer, who encouraged Mengele to utilize the Auschwitz children.

The grouping of Josef Mengele's research by educational criteria meant that any government oversight was nonexistent, and Mengele's desire to out-research his colleagues led him to bend the rules of acceptability. — All personal feelings should be forgotten in consultations, the good of the patients ought to be the chief and only consideration. In each case during this period, the German state superseded the patient, oftentimes to the detriment of the infirmed. Furthermore, the demarcation of another set of guidelines removed any oversight.

These guidelines were as follows:

> *...distinguished explicitly between therapeutic and non-therapeutic research. Without exception, nontherapeutic studies could be conducted only with the subject's formal informed consent. Therapeutic research, however, was possible without consent in a medical emergency and if deemed in the patient's best interest. These categorizations were open for interpretation by the researchers.*

Josef Mengele ensured the categorization of his research as therapeutic, thereby eliminating the necessity of informed consent. By arguing the research was for the betterment of the German state in general and that his findings would ease the pain of the German people, Mengele was roundly supported by the Nazi government. The categorical language was ambiguous specifically so that it would be interpreted by the practitioner in a manner that best suited the experiment.

The Hippocratic maxim of 'do no harm' seemingly would invalidate Mengele's Auschwitz research. It is vitally important, however, not to impose the professional ethics of modern society on research conducted seventy years ago. To Josef Mengele, 'do no harm' was quite applicable to Auschwitz. The overriding German anti-Semitism which existed promoted treating the Jews not as human beings, with the requisite respect for the person, but rather as an infestation or disease. "Out of respect for human life, I would remove a purulent appendix from a diseased body. The Jew is the purulent appendix in the body of Europe.

This sentiment is mirrored by many physicians who participated in the Holocaust, who were questioned on how they justified these actions. Illustrating the common mentality, historian Ihor Kamenetsky quietly responded with "When you find diseased appendix, you must remove it". Ultimately, the categorization of a race as subhuman removes any concern regarding what is considered murder.

Legislative actions passed in prior years, specifically those enacted against the Jewish populations, allowed for such an environment. The mass killing of the jews was more akin to pest extermination... than to killing human beings. Evolvingprofessional medical ethics did not allow for even a paternalistic protection of the so-called subspecies. This mind frame is difficult to understand today, but the current ethical code would be equally foreign to Josef Mengele. Despite the subhuman categorization, the Nazi doctors still sought professional justification for the Auschwitz research. This was not a result of some altruistic concern for the patient. Rather, it was a front to show the Red Cross that each examination and experiment was ethically conducted. Even selection was administered in such a way that it appeared medically legitimate. Since no medical examinations at the selection ramp were done and no medical skill was required for this function, theNazis apparently sought to invest it with medical authority and represent it as a medical procedure. Even more than simply appealing for Red Cross validity, there was a practical reason for this behavior as it prevented prisoner revolt. Whereas the inmates inside the barbed wires had been systematically stripped of humanity, and likewise their resistance, the captives emerging from the cattle cars were slightly healthier and could be physically able to resist.

While not at their peak strength, owing to several days in the transport cars, these inmates could reasonably become volatile once aware of the camp conditions. After the selection, the same SS doctor would enter the ambulance-like vehicle with a red cross and together with the SDG (a medical technician) ride to the gas chamber. At the gas chamber, the gas would be administered under the doctor's technical supervision. The charade continued to the very end; inmates were permitted to log their suitcases and personal effects in preparation for retrieval. After the gas chamber doors were locked, the *sonderkommando* would enter and remove all personal items to Kanada, the location where the contents were cataloged and valuables dispersed throughout Germany.

The twisted truism of 'do no harm' seems to be the ultimate maxim under which the Nazi medical leaders operated. The war provided the front by which the social disease was removed to better the lives of the German people and the Reich. Another more significant level of medicalized killing was the idea of killing as a therapeutic imperative. Years of economic depression and disruption led to unrest, and it became a healing mechanism to blame, and ultimately murder, the Jews for their culpability.

It is important to note that Josef Mengele believed his actions to be ethical and, under German law, he committed no actual crimes in Auschwitz. Nazi dogma viewed the changing landscape and the coming victory in the Second World War as the advent of a new civilization, and this revolution would forever change the medical profession. Away with all that is unfit to live, for the restoration of a sound and healthy people.Away with all the biologically inferior, forward to a new biological superiority. The elimination of those unworthy of life would help create a new Aryan world order in which physician-approved legislation would determine who is fit to live.

The Nazis were notorious for selecting key passages from ethical codes and amending each as justification for Auschwitz. There was a mercy killing dimension in all this, a kind of pseudo-Nietzschean expression of will toward asserting the most powerful and strong elements in the race while getting rid of the weak elements. Josef Mengele's experiments were not simply a singular crime rooted in anti-Semitism or psychosis. His ethical construct was the result of an education strengthened in German universities, where he was introduced to the ethics of racial hygienics.

Ingrained in Mengele was more than simply eradicating a world pest, it was a noble stand of defiance. The Jews held high ranking positions in industry and banking, but it was theorized that this success would still not satisfy the voracious Jewish appetite for power. The Protocols of Zion mandated a new Jewish global leadership, and Mengele was taught that this revolution would begin with the eradication of the German intelligentsia. The Nazi doctors blamed the victim in many ways. They blamed the jews for being non-human, for being the threatening factor. Mengele saw that unlocking the programmability of twin reproduction was paramount in preventing the German demise.

Another unethical means by which the Auschwitz doctors were killed was the refusal of treatment. With the imprisonment of over one hundred thousand malnourished and ill-treated persons, communicable diseases decimated the population. An outbreak of cholera or typhus, of which several occurred, could not only wipe out the slave labor supporting the war effort but also could threaten to disrupt the camp‘s infrastructure.

Doctors also conducted a form of murderous epidemiology by wiping outwards or people when they became ill with an epidemic condition like typhus. Josef Mengele successfully charted a strategy and its implementation prevented an outbreak of typhus in the women‘s camp. His method, unfortunately, called for eliminating one entire bank of women captives. Mengele ordered for roughly three thousand women to be immediately gassed. The bunk was cleaned, and after delousing, residents of a separate bunk took in their new residence. The vacated bunk was cleaned and freshly delouse prisoners were moved in and the process continued. By ordering the gassing of a few thousand innocent women, Josef Mengele received a commendation for his efforts.

In the presence of close family and friends, Mengele could be loving and tender. Moreover, he exhibited normal benevolent professional behavior in the camp by providing chocolates to the children and aiding a pregnant prisoner through tough labor. Conversely, when agitated, Mengele exhibited characteristics of psychotic doubling. — On the one hand, Mengele had normal human feelings. He had befriended this inmate doctor... he would save a drowning gypsy, give him medication, keep him alive — only the next moment to send him to the gas chamber. Whatever his mental state, the deadly actions were still, by German law, ethical practices. The evil face of Mengele's killing personality was cognizant of the era‘s legislation. Simply put,

Mengele was acutely aware of the new role of ethics in his profession. He previously helped to develop legislation built upon the ethical foundations he learned in German universities.

Historians thoroughly researched the complicity of the medical profession in Nazi war crimes and insist that there were never any protests from the highly compromised medical elite against such atrocities and that after the war careers continued with no sense of having violated medical ethics. It is inaccurate to assume the Nazi physicians discarded long-held ethical beliefs in Auschwitz. Each trial and study was well within the state-mandated guidelines. An SS colleague of Mengele's was quoted as saying that "...ethics was not a word used in Auschwitz. Doctors and others spoke only about how to do things most efficiently, about what worked best.

A cold and emotionless medical environment came to dominate Germany and within the confines of Auschwitz, this setting became normal. A difficulty in applying ethics to Josef Mengele is avoiding the temptation of utilizing constructs that were not available before 1945. Any attempt to retroactively analyze Mengele's experiments in such a way would be disingenuous. However, there are four main ethical principles of which Josef Mengele most likely had intimate knowledge. These four main principles are:

1. Nonmaleficence – from the Hippocratic writings we have retained the maxim "First of all, do no harm". This remains an important principle, though it is well recognized that virtually no treatment options are free from potentially harmful side effects.
2. Beneficence – we should do what is in the patient's best interests.
3. Autonomy – patients have a right to make their own decisions about medical treatment.

4. Justice – we should treat patients without favoritism or discrimination. Thus, if two patients have a similar condition, we should offer the same recommendations and treatments to them rather than giving preference to one or the other based on status or our potentially biased assessment of them.

The Nazis altered the nonmaleficence ethics of bullet point number one by posturing that allowing the Jewish race to live would be doing irreparable harm to the global society. However, Nazi dogmatic ideals cannot validate experiments with bullet points two through four. It is not in a child's best interest to remove pre-pubescent testicles or to be injected with typhus. The Auschwitz children did not have the autonomy to research and authorize any experiment, nor did their guardians. Finally, Mengele operated with extreme degrees of favoritism and preference. A child emerging from the transport car who was not part of a set of twins was selected to go directly to the gas-chamber. Moreover, as seen with Joe Rosenblum, Josef Mengele would protect any child if they provided a valuable service.

Professional ethics has strong roots in the Golden Rule. The logical result of practicing the Golden Rule is an increase in the overall societal good. Realistically, it is too simplistic to label the Holocaust as unethical in this prism. Through the eyes of the German public, who had endured an embarrassing defeat in World War I and suffered through the economic wasteland that was the Weimar Republic, blame fell entirely to the Jews. In Nazi Germany in the 1930s and 1940s, it would have been inconceivable to apply the Golden Rule to European Jews. Furthermore, the Golden Rule could not apply to Jews as they were not legally considered human.

Another foundation for medical ethics is the ideal care for the individual. Using the Jews as research subjects only causes injustice to the patient. The patient's best interests were not being identified and protected in Auschwitz, as Jewish inmates were routinely denied proper medical care. These necessities were refused not because of an actual crime, but because of Nazi racism. On this view, determining that someone should not receive care because species-typical functioning cannot be achieved for them would be to deepen the injustice.... On this basis, it would be discriminatory.

Again, eliminating the Jews protected the state, and the German state was of the utmost importance.

One principle goal of medicine is to prevent disease. Each physician has "an almost sacred duty to combat all known causes of death". Yet in Auschwitz, many known causes of death were permitted to flourish. Overworked and malnourished, Auschwitz prisoners went through their daily routine of back-breaking labor, poor sanitation, and severe beatings at the hands of the SS. No aid was administered to a prisoner who contracted typhus or dysentery. Likewise, no aid was administered in the event of a broken bone or another physical malady. The inmate was typically executed and another prisoner was inserted into the role.

Informed consent requires attention to two basic components: the nature of the study, the procedures to be administered, the risks and potential benefits if any, alternatives to participation, and the right to decline or withdraw participation without penalty. Second, subjects must voluntarily agree to participate under these conditions. Mengele did not provide his test subjects with the opportunity to research his test, nor did he obtain signed informed consent from a guardian. Mengele also did not arrange to provide suitable accommodations for post-surgery recovery and failed to provide adequate trial information to even his closest colleagues. Furthermore, there are several key provisions that protect involvement in a clinical study, as follows:

> *These include procedures to protect privacy and confidentiality, monitoring the condition of research subjects to assure their safety, terminating study participation in the case of adverse events, and informing enrolled subjects about risks and benefits discovered in the course of research...*

The camp's children were not treated in a manner consistent with these provisions. Even the camp infirmary was commonly referred to as the waiting room for the gas chamber. Nazi racial hygienics would argue that these provisions have no bearing on Jewish subjects. Due to the passing of several race laws, Jews were not treated as humans, and once a human being has been stripped of his human and given a para-anthropoid identity, the normal moral impediments cease to operate. Again, viewing Jews as subhuman was not a new idea. The belief was reinforced over many years and this belief was deeply ingrained in German society, but this categorization prevented the ethical treatment of Jewish patients.

Josef Mengele's professional aspirations drove him to Auschwitz, as he saw the opportunity to autopsy fresh corpses as the medical breakthrough he needed. Mengele, and his contemporaries, were attracted to the Nazi party by promises that the National Socialists will remove the Jewish predominance from the profession (60% of the physicians in Berlin were Jewish) and restore the prestige, honor, and dignity of the Aryan physicians. By eliminating professional colleagues, Mengele's could now apply for many different open positions that were previously unavailable. Therefore, his professional ambitions could more easily be realized.

The war-crimes trial in Nuremberg highlighted a disconcerting reality regarding the medical profession. Testimony showed that the medical profession lacked a written *charta*, a statement of principles professing its traditional ethos, which had been deemed self-understood and sufficient. Before the establishment of the Declaration of Geneva in 1948, German physicians were free to operate by whatever ethical code best suited the experiment. It was common to see these codes amended depending on the study.

The change in philosophy meant that the Nazi state was infinitely more important than the individual. One of the more influential factors was a significant shift in perspective from the emphasis on the care and cure of the individual and the community to the treatment|| of the body politic as a whole. German physicians eagerly modified their practices to align with this new paradigm. In doing so, German research is fostered not by the paternalistic care and protection of subhumans, but rather by utilizing Jews as a disposable commodity in improving Aryan life. the Nuremberg Tribunal acknowledged that scientists justified human experiments on the basis that they yield results for the good of human society that could not be produced by other means of study. The ascension of German academia to global esteem would be borne on the back of human test subjects. These subjects would allow for immeasurable research and a new enlightened era would emerge.

This fundamental emotive change in German society is paramount. The new Aryan-German citizen was hard working and tough. Generosity and compassion for others had fostered a weak society unable to emerge victorious from World War I. Full devotion to the Aryan platform and callous disregard for outsiders became commonplace. The snowballing fanaticism was not exclusive to the German military; it also permeated the medical field. Whereas physicians generally perceive the preservation of life as their prime goal, death had become a core value in their overall belief system. Death had become synonymous with progress, and experimenting on the inmate children was only the means to an end. Complicating the issue was the fact that there existed no international consensus among doctors about the use of humans in experimental research. This resulted in an unfortunate environment of promoting the state's needs to the detriment of the patient‘s best needs.

The cultural shift resulted from decades of war failure, economic devastation,anti-Semitism, and fear-mongering. As Germany struggled to recover, the race laws enacted by Hitler mirrored societal trends. Certain rights were restricted by the government, which was allowed to overstep its bounds by a frustrated public. In times of war, government modifies its sovereignty by overriding the legal system and exerting power on human beings who cease to be citizens protected by civil rights and are now seen as biological units. Under extreme duress, national governments are often allowed to take an increased role in a citizen‘s life, even to the detriment of civil rights.

Josef Mengele‘s experiments, while unacceptable, did ultimately lead to the international establishment of a professional code of ethics. There have been substantive measures taken to ensure another medical Holocaust is prevented.

> *The experiment must be scientific, not a random game of trial and error. It must be based on a sound protocol with the area of inquiry, the hypothesis, and the nature of the clinical tryout so well defined that the need for using human subjects is demonstrated. Normally, this means that earlier scientific investigations, including tryouts on animals, preceded clinical research on human subjects.*

The Declaration of Geneva was the important first step in protecting patient‘s rights. The current ethical landscape owes its strictness to physicians such as Josef Mengele, however disturbing it is to give him a certain modicum of credit. As for the dilemma on whether to use

Mengele's research, most appropriately when he writes that by using the data without the consent of those who were violated is to violate the violated anew.

Furthermore, many Jewish historians and survivors have commented on this ethical predicament. As representatives of those most directly affected by the Holocaust, each is an important voice in answering this very question.

The issue of whether to use the Nazi data is a smokescreen from the reality of human suffering. Instead of the word "data", I suggest that we replace it with an Auschwitz bar of soap. This horrible bar of soap is the remains of murdered Jews. The image sensitizes and personalizes our dilemma. Imagine the extreme feeling of discomfort and the mortified look of horror upon discovering that one just showered with the remains of murdered Jews. The ghastly thought of Nazismelting human beings (and perhaps even one's close relatives) together for a bar of soap precludes any consideration of its use. How could any civilized person divorce the horror from the carnage without numbing one's self to the screams of the tortured and ravaged faces of the Holocaust? Indeed it is only with this enhanced sensitivity to the suffering that one can accurately deal with the Nazi "data".

CHAPTER V

APPLYING ETHICAL THEORIES TO NAZISM

Aristotle (384 BC – 322 BC) is widely considered one of the most influential philosophers in recorded history. His writings have created an entire discipline of published literature in philosophy, ethics, and more. While he lived and died thousands of years before Josef Mengele, Aristotle's influence still permeated German social ethics of the early twentieth century. By analyzing the philosophy behind the social changes in Nazi Germany, I hope to answer the question of whether it is ethical to use Mengele's research.

Aristotle does not specifically address the ethical question of state-sponsored genocide in his writings. He does, however, address certain behaviors perpetrated by the Nazis in their push for European supremacy. Scholars and modern philosophers routinely attempt to apply Aristotle's philosophy to World War II, and a prominent scholar, Lloyd Gerson, argues that the largest obstacle Aristotle would see with state-sponsored genocide is that he does not believe nation-states should operate as moral entities.

> *The mistake is to suppose that nations are moral agents. If one supposes this, then whatever theory of morality one wishes to defend, one will assume that that theory applies to nations. Thus, if one, say, defends a version of utilitarianism or some sort of deontological theory, one will then go on to claim its applicability to nations, treating them as if they were moral agents.*

Therefore, states should not intervene in the affairs of other nation-states, such as occupying Austria or invading Poland, even if the government believes the intentions to be righteous. Gerson believes that Aristotle would argue Germany should not concern itself with the ethnic affairs in Europe or with being an Aryan bulwark in the racial struggle.

Gerson concludes that Aristotle would approve of a nation acting as a legitimate international agent as long as the nation does not violently impose its moral beliefs on its neighbors. Subsequently, this author believes Aristotle would argue that the final solution should never have been authorized, as Nazi Germany had no moral right to forcefully evacuate Jews from sovereign European countries. Aristotle would have disapproved of German expansion under the guise of finding adequate living space for ethnic Germans. This lebensraum initiative included acts of violence and mayhem against Germany's neighbors. Aristotle writes that "...the political life entails the just treatment of foreigners and fellow citizens alike."

Predating the later creation of concentration and forced labor camps, early measures enacted by Hitler's government violated several sovereign nations" autonomy and are thusly unethical.

However, that is not to say Aristotle is opposed to political change. Allowing for the rise of the Nazi Party, Aristotle would argue that if a system is unjust or unfair, itis morally appropriate to amend a government's constitution. "Aristotle makes it clear that a subjective feeling of injustice is sufficient as a cause of dissidence...."

The inequities of the Treaty of Versailles and the financial ruin suffered under the Weimar Republic were seen as adequate justification for the Nazi ascension to power.

Aristotle could have agreed that the dire financial and social depression in Germany during the 1920s and 1930s were substantial motivations for political change. This is not to say that Aristotle would have supported Nazism, simply that political change was warranted because the Weimar Republic was failing. When analyzing Josef Mengele through the prism of ethical theories, one must determine why Utilitarianism is ideal. There exist many different theories that could be utilized to determine whether one's behavior is ethical. These include the golden rule, which states that you must do unto others only as you would have them do unto you. Kant's Categorical Imperative states that you should only act in a way that you would be willing to see become universal law. The Revelation Ethic of the modern philosophical era encourages one to pray, to whichever god the individual believes in, for support and guidance4. However, for Mengele's purpose, the Utilitarian Principle is preferable:

> *The principle of utilitarianism is, therefore, a consequential principle, or as stated earlier a teleological principle. In its simplest form, utilitarianism asserts that "we should always act to produce the greatest ratio of good to evil for everyone" ...one should take that course of action that represents the "greatest good for the greatest number".*

Utilitarianism is the ethic by which the Nazi Party justified the Holocaust. Therefore, itis justice to use this same principle in analyzing Josef Mengele. Mengele was likely aware of his era's predominant professional ethics. With the intense and extensive education he received in Germany, he very likely would also have been cognizant of the popular ethical theories and how they related to the rising Nazi party. Opponents of Nazi party politics would have argued that the National Socialist politics were in stark violation of utilitarianism. However, as seen previously, the Nazis skewed Utilitarianism so that it actually supported the party's aims and means. Thereafter, once in power, the Nazis began a secret process of eliminating those considered unfit to live. A program was enacted to systematically murder the mentally handicapped and physically deformed.

There is an argument within Utilitarianism that supports eliminating the weaker societal elements. This, in part, states:

1. The morally right thing to do, on any occasion, is whatever would bring about the greatest balance of happiness over unhappiness.
2. On at least some occasions, the greatest balance of happiness over unhappiness may be brought about by mercy killing.
3. Therefore, on at least some occasions, mercy killing may be morally right.

It is this last Utilitarian point, stating that mercy killings may actually be morally right, which could have encouraged the Nazis to pursue systematic liquidation. However, this author believes that the definition of "mercy killing" in this passage refers to ending the life of someone gravely suffering from a terminal disease or condition, and not exterminating the Jews, the handicapped, and others under the political motivations of the Third Reich. Therefore, any justification of euthanasia or "mercy killing" using Utilitarianism is erroneous.

The Nazis began to integrate decades of Social Darwinist writings into their legislation and Hitler, as the party leader, began to pass measures aimed at curtailing the liberties of the sub-species, Jews and Gypsies especially, because he believed each to bean unacceptable existence. Hitler considered them inferior beings that before the advent of Christian and humanitarian ethics would have died out in the struggle for existence. Hitler even signed a document freeing physicians from legal prosecution if they committed mercy killings, even though this act was still technically illegal under German law.

It is possible to refute Utilitarianism using an alternative ethical theory. The theory of Professional Ethics states that one "...should only do that which can be explained before a committee of your peers." In this case, the coworkers of the Nazi Party happen to be Mengele's peers. These colleagues supported his research regardless of its violent human rights violations. Through the cold eyes of German physicians, the utilization of murder was not ideal, but the results were necessary to establish a greater Germany. By applying this principle, one could argue that it was ethical for the German government to support Mengele"s research, and his behavior was likely politically supported. However, it is the opinion of this author that the application of Utilitarianism must include Jews, Slavs, and Gypsies among the "greater good" and therefore is more relevant than the Professional Ethics theory.

The German Social Darwinist ideal of "survival of the fittest" increasingly gained popularity and combined with other ethical doctrines, such as those which state that in assessing consequences, the only that thing that matters is the amount of happiness or unhappiness that is caused. Everything else is irrelevant. Thus right actions are those that produce the greatest balance of happiness over unhappiness.

The question of Jewish happiness was not a matter for German ethicists or leaders. Viewed as subhuman, the only concern was for those considered Aryan or "good".The struggle for Aryan supremacy was a fight based on philosophical beliefs:

> *As Darwinists consistently taught, the struggle for existence necessarily resulted in mass death for the "unfit," which caused evolutionary progress. Hitler –along with some other Darwinists – believed that the right to life only belonged to the "fit," which they interpreted as the healthy and strong.*

Hitler blamed Christian ideals for the social aversion to murdering the weaker elements of society. He blamed western philosophy for engendering a belief in the "right to life"" for all human beings. Hitler argued that, as within the animal kingdom, there exists a hierarchy amongst humans and that some are more important to preserve than others. Here Hitler clearly expressed his belief that the evolutionary struggle should eliminate all humanitarian considerations, including the conception of a natural right to life for all humans, which was a fundamental element of Western human rights philosophy.

This changing philosophy took the bite out of killing, it took the guilt out of beating an elderly individual, and it took the stigma away from being violent. As it was all part and parcel of the evolutionary process, it became acceptable and honorable. Backed by Nazi dogma, killing became accepted normative behavior. It became unacceptable to allow for the degenerate to live and unthinkable to allow the degenerate to procreate. No condition that would possibly present a danger of degeneracy was to be overlooked, and it was considered a patriotic duty of all Germans to watch over the health and purity of their offspring. German scientists and intellectuals began to produce literature that promoted this belief and promulgated the acceptability of murder. While Josef Mengele"s doctoral work did not show any overt sense of racism, it mirrored the belief that heredity alone determines whether one was fit to live.

Without any evidence, scientists concluded that human differences were hereditary and unalterable, and in doing so, they "precluded redemption" because they imposed "the additional burden of intrinsic inferiority upon despised groups." While Kant would argue that each person"s rights are paramount and should not be violated, the GermanNazi government and medical elite worked in tandem to create a society in which murder was more than just acceptable, it was philosophically just. This is the society in which Josef Mengele was educated and encouraged to make his mark on history.

Subsequently, the question remains on how to utilize the data amassed by theNazis in research conducted in the present day. Understandably, this is an uneasy subject, but the ethical arguments are available to form a definitive conclusion.

The first argument in support of using Mengele"s research states that while how his research was obtained was wholly deplorable, the information still exists and therefore should be used to increase the overall health. Furthermore, the Nazi data can be used so long as the purpose is an important one, and the data is presented with a clear moral denunciation of how it was obtained. Perhaps the opinions of ethical theorists, survivors, and historians would differ greatly if the research unlocked the cure for a major disease. For example, if theNazis discovered a cure for cancer, then in that case it would be ethically responsible to utilize the data. However, the Nazis did not discover a cure for cancer and so this argument is irrelevant.

To accuse a present-day physician of condoning Mengele"s research and as complicit in the Nazi holocaust due to the use of data is unfair and inaccurate. It is entirely unreasonable to suggest that by using Nazi data, scientists become party to the evil of Dachau. By analogy, a physician who makes use of the body of a murder victim or an aborted fetus is neither a murderer nor an abortionist. Researchers who would utilize the Nazi research do not necessarily agree with the methods by which the information was obtained. However unfortunate the circumstance, the information still exists and should be available for use if it will better the collective health of humans.

Conversely, ethics will argue that the research was stolen and unethical in its original nature, and therefore should be banished from use. The data should be condemned to oblivion and never used by science, although the descriptions of the experiments can be republished as a reminder of the Nazi horror. Because of the depravity with which the research was obtained, any use of that data would be inflicting more injury and offense to every victim of the Holocaust. Concentration camp survivors have even expressed opinions on the matter. Rose Kaplovitz, a camp survivor, states that "... she did not want to see the data used because no one should be indebted to the Nazis." This is not to say that the medical complicity in the Holocaust should be ignored; only that the research should not be used as a source in the present day.

Furthermore, the Nazi data has been stolen through forced extraction from the bodies of the Jews, so that if anyone should control the data's use, it should be the Jews themselves. They have the right, then, to insist that the data not be used, because the data was pillaged from their ravaged bodies alone. There has been no documentation of Jewish groups expressing favor of utilizing the Nazi research. As are presentation of the ethnicity most gravely affected by the concentration camps, this denouncement must be acknowledged and heeded.

The evolving political, professional, and deontological structure of Germany after World War I allowed for the creation of camps such as Auschwitz. Furthermore, institutionalized murder was accepted, facilitated, and promoted by the medical community. Moreover, the entire philosophical subject of Social Darwinism was conspicuously absent from British and German deontological literature until the end of World War II. Therefore, any international pressure to halt this murderous new system was nonexistent. Thankfully, following World War II, the Allied Powers were determined to prevent another medically-induced Holocaust from reoccurring.

Subsequently, a system of statutes collectively called the Nuremberg Code was passed shortly after the end of the war. It details a strict system of medical assurances that are concrete and leave nothing open to interpretation or abuse. It states, in part:

1. The voluntary consent of the human subject is absolutely essential. This means that the person involved should have the legal capacity to give consent; should be so situated as to be able to exercise free power of choice, without the intervention of any element of force/fraud, deceit, duress, overreaching, or other ulterior form of constraint or coercion; and should have sufficient knowledge and comprehension of the elements of the subject matter involved as to enable him to make an understanding and enlightened decision. This latter element requires that before the acceptance of an affirmative decision by the experimental subject there should be made known to him the nature, duration, and purpose of the experiment; the method and means by; which it is to be conducted; all inconveniences and hazards reasonably to be expected; and the effects upon his health or person which may possibly come from his participation in the experiment. The duty and responsibility for ascertaining the quality of the consent rests upon each individual who, initiates, directs, or engages in the experiment. It is a personal duty and responsibility which may not be delegated to another with impunity.
2. The experiment should be such as to yield fruitful results for the good of society, unprocurable by other methods or means of study, and not random and unnecessary in nature.
3. The experiment should be so designed and based on the results of animal experimentation and a knowledge of the natural history of the disease or other problem under study that the anticipated results will justify the performance of the

experiment.

4. The experiment should be so conducted as to avoid all unnecessary physical and mental suffering and injury.
5. No experiment should be conducted where there is an a priori reason to believe that death or disabling injury will occur; except, perhaps, in those experiments where the experimental physicals also serve as subjects.
6. The degree of risk to be taken should never exceed that determined by the humanitarian importance of the problem to be solved by the experiment.
7. Proper preparations should be made and adequate facilities provided to protect the experimental subject against even remote possibilities of injury, disability, or death.
8. The experiment should be conducted only by scientifically qualified persons.
9. The highest degree of skill and care should be required through all stages of the experiment of those who conduct or engage in the experiment.
10. During the course of the experiment, the human subject should be at liberty to bring the experiment to an end if he has reached the physical or mental state where continuation of the experiment seems to him to be impossible.
11. During the course of the experiment, the scientist in charge must be prepared to terminate the experiment at any stage if he has probable cause to believe, in the exercise of good faith, superior skill, and careful judgment required of him, that a continuation of the experiment is likely to result in injury, disability, or death to the experimental subject.

As difficult as it is to give credit to Josef Mengele, his atrocious behavior helped directly lead to the world of today, where patient rights are protected and abuse is limited. In conclusion, most ethical theories, when applied to Josef Mengele, would disapprove of the means by which he amassed his data. Furthermore, these theories, combined with survivor statements, arrive at a single conclusion; Josef Mengele'sresearch was conducted unethically. Even with taking Stephen Post"s point of view into consideration, this author believes that the utilization of Nazi research in modern medical trials would be entirely unethical due to the nature by which the research was conducted.

CHAPTER VI

MENGELE'S COLLEAGUES IN AUSCHWITZ

The horrific experience of Auschwitz did not consist solely of Josef Mengele"s experiments. Auschwitz I, Auschwitz II – Birkenau, and Auschwitz III – Monowitz all combined to hold upwards of one hundred thousand souls from all over Europe. Many inhabitants never came into contact with Josef Mengele, but their experiences were no less gruesome. This chapter will describe Josef Mengele"s medical colleagues, as well as give a rough overview of concentration camp life.

The original deployment of Nazi physicians to Auschwitz was perhaps a welcoming sight to the initial Polish and Russian prisoners of the concentration camp.

However, this excitement was quickly erased when the inmates realized that the physicians were not there to keep the prisoners healthy, but rather to conduct heinous experiments in the name of Nazi science. Realistically, the physicians were deployed to Auschwitz for two main reasons. The first reason included discovering new ways of curing disease, programming German reproduction, and helping German soldiers endure extreme conditions on the war front. The second reason was to facilitate the systematic murder of Auschwitz's inmates. The SS doctor did no direct medical work. His primary function was to carry out Auschwitz's institutional program of medicalized genocide.

Nazi physicians were encouraged to conduct limitless research trials due to the innumerable test subjects. However, even with unfettered access to research subjects and no adherence to medical ethics, nothing substantial ever emerged from the physicians "work.

While Auschwitz was one of the largest concentration camps, and certainly the one in which the most Jews were murdered, it was not the first concentration camp to employ doctors among the inmates. The medical blocks probably existed because of prior concentration camp practice, concern about epidemics, and above all the broad Nazi impulse toward medical legitimation of killing. The combination of the Nazi drive for medical professional elitism and the availability of test subjects, sprinkled with the fear of typhus and dysentery, provided the perfect storm for the medical deployment to the Polish countryside. Auschwitz would soon stand alone as the most diabolical Nazi beacon of Aryan science and power.

In contrast to the Nazi ideal of superiority, the actual physicians who were conscripted to work in the camps were not, in mass, the medical elite. Of course, there were renowned physicians and researchers in their midst, such as Josef Mengele, but the general practitioners in the camps were rather unremarkable. The SS doctors assigned to the concentration camps tended to be medically undistinguished, strong in their Nazi ties, and personally self-aggrandizing.

This led to a majority of the experiments being conducted rather shoddily by those professionals who had no business operating in that discipline. Unfortunately, this unprofessionalism also led to a rampant increase in patient suffering.

With the research largely resulting in the death of the test subject, the Nazi physicians organized a way to catalog each death using natural causes. Doctors authorized false death certificates, attributing each death of an Auschwitz inmate or an outsider brought there to be killed to a specific illness (cardiac, respiratory, infectious, or whatever). It is important to note that those prisoners unloaded from the transport cars and sent directly to the gas chambers were never entered into the camp's registrar and therefore no alternative cause of death was necessary.

These lower-tier medical professionals were also responsible for administering selection on a daily basis. More than that, however, the doctors were involved in the entire killing process, from the transport car to the gas chambers. Their participation was as follows:

> *...first, the chief doctor's assignments to his subordinates concerning duty schedules and immediate selection policies; second, the individual doctor's service on the ramp, performing selections in a very noble seemingly kind manner; third, the doctor riding in the ambulance or Red Cross car to the crematoria; fourth, the doctor ordering how many pellets of gas should be thrown in these holes from the ceilings, according to the number of people, and who should do it.... There were three or four Desinfektoren; fifth, he observed through the hole how the people are dying; sixth, when the people were dead, he gave the order to ventilate to open the gas chamber, and he came with a gas mask into the chamber; seventh, he signed a form that the people are dead and how long it took; and eighth, he observed the teeth extraction from the corpses.*

This was done primarily to trick the prisoners into walking towards the gas chambers without inciting violence or revolt. Impeccably dressed, the doctors were respected and trusted by the new inmates. This mirage was intentional and highly successful in keeping order during the unloading chaos. It would be inappropriate to simply categorize every Nazi physician as an uneducated and myopic believer in the acceptability of murder and human suffering. There did exist physicians working in Auschwitz who was highly regarded before the war. One of the most important and tireless reporters on the Auschwitz concentration camp, Hermann Langbein, approached the categorization question and was ultimately able to classify the Nazi doctors as follows:

> *...zealots who participated eagerly in the extermination process and even did "extra work" on behalf of killing; those who went about the process more or less methodically and did no more and no less than they felt they had to do; and those who participated in the extermination process only reluctantly.*

There are examples of doctors helping inmates to better medical care or extra rations of food. However, this seems to be the exception rather than the rule. Furthermore, it was not professionally advantageous for the doctors to act in such a beneficent manner while employed in the concentration camp. German accolades and promotions were only given to those doctors who most closely followed Nazi protocol, not those who aided in keeping a prisoner out of the gas chambers. The highest German military honor was bestowed upon only a few men in Auschwitz: the recipients were Otto Moll, who was in charge of the gas chambers; Josef Klehr, who administered the largest number of poison injections and later became chief of the "disinfectors", who had to insert the poison gas; and Hoss himself. These decorations were an unmistakable indication that Himmler approved of the three men's zeal, and at the same time, it underscored the fiction that mass murder in Auschwitz was the equivalent of frontline service.

The overall intention of the Auschwitz concentration camp was the medical justification of human experimentation and murder. Those who adhered to this policy with the utmost fervor were celebrated and promoted. This established an environment of increasing violence and suffering among the prisoners. A unique problem that the Auschwitz doctors encountered was how to deal with camp pregnancies. Typically, a pregnant mother was immediately gassed along with her unborn child. However, some women were able to escape imminent death during selection and in the following months went into labor. Standard medical ethics state that if a mother and child are in peril during the birthing process, the mother must be saved first. In Auschwitz, this extended to immediately after the birth, even if the child was born healthy. Lucie Adelsberger, a prisoner physician, worked extensively with pregnant women while imprisoned in Auschwitz. Unfortunately, she writes that the newborn had to die immediately if the mother's life were to be saved. Sympathetic prisoner doctors "...saved up all the poison we could find in the camp and it still wasn't enough. It's amazing what newborns can bear. They simply slept off otherwise lethal doses of poison without any apparent damage."

In some cases, the child's life was spared and the birth was hidden. However, in most cases, the child was either killed by the SS or the mother chose to walk with her newborn into the gas chambers because she refused to be separated.

One of the more ruthless Auschwitz physicians was Dr. Freidrich Entress, who became an expert at administering phenol injections directly into the heart cavity, which would cause almost immediate death. Dr. Entress is one of the doctors that Hermann Langbein would have categorized as one of the zealots who did extra work to curry favor with his SS superiors. In fact, Dr. Entress took a routine order from the Auschwitz Central Office as an excuse to increase his killing capabilities. He soon pioneered the use of phenol injections in the infirmary, which was previously unknown to that extent, and organized it in such a way that any of the ss medics to whom Entress soon entrusted this dirty work could easily and without a hitch kill a hundred or more patients utilizing phenol injections.

This deadly work could be concluded in the matter of a few short hours, and by lunch, the former patients were burning in the crematorium. Dr. Entress was also responsible for the infirmary selections conducted to prevent overcrowding in the hospital. Entress would routinely order the patient to strip naked before his arrival, and then Entress would only give a cursory peek at the patient before making his decision. Entress contented himself with just glancing at the naked patients presented to him in the clinic before he made the decision. However, he reported to Wirths that all those he had destined for death had tuberculosis.

Because the Nazi authorities did not question "tuberculosis" as an ailment and desperately wished to avoid a tuberculosis outbreak, the categorization of this illness was not questioned and Entress was permitted to continue with his selections.

Another infamous Auschwitz physician was Professor Carl Clauberg, who experimented with ways of sterilizing the Jewish population. Heinrich Himmler had been searching for a way to effectively sterilize the entire population, as systematic liquidation of the Jewish people was proving somewhat ineffective and labor-intensive.

Clauberg was to find an answer to a question that occupied the heads of all concentration and extermination camps: how can offensive peoples still be eradicated while still making use of their labor for the arms industry? As the German war effort became increasingly bereft of men and munitions, the need for a slave labor force increased. Whereas a principal goal of concentration camps had been to forcefully exterminate those considered subhuman, this was amended to include a workforce producing wartime commodities. In fact, the third sub-camp of Auschwitz, called Auschwitz III – Monowitz, was an IG Farben production plant for synthetic rubber, commonly referred to as Buna.

Clauberg routinely injected mixtures into a woman's womb to produce sterility but his colleague Dr. Horst Schumann experimented freely on both women and men to increase a population's sterility. Differing from Clauberg in his methods, Schumann routinely utilized radiation as the means for sterilization, considered an extremely painful procedure. Furthermore, Schumann had no professional training in radiation treatment. During his trial following the war, Schumann acknowledged in court that he had no psychiatric training that would have enabled him to judgemental illnesses; and when he began his series of experiments in Auschwitz, he did not know any more than that about radiation treatment.

Dr. Schumann is emblematic of the Nazi environment in that he was not trained in the specific discipline he was responsible for; rather, he was simply an SS doctor who was willing to radiate the genitals of men and women and seemed to suffer no ill mental effects from the responsibility.

A general concern in the Nazi infirmary was that some members of the slave labor force were intentionally becoming ill to avoid the harshest work. This manner of escaping service was also present in the Wehrmacht (German Armed Forces), which was losing numbers at an astounding rate. Ultimately, it fell to Dr. Emil Kaschub to devise an experiment that would best determine if the infirmed was legitimately ill or if the illness was faked. Through subcutaneous injections and ointments, pus, sewage, and unknown chemicals – [Emil] Kaschub gave his test subjects cellulitis, which he repeatedly photographed and lanced.

Due to the malaise within the German army, the doctors in Auschwitz were hopeful of creating an experiment that would decrease the number of Wehrmacht patients. That experiment was created and fostered in the flesh of Auschwitz prisoners, but it was ultimately unsuccessful.

While Dr. Entress frequently only glanced at his patients during selection, the majority of Auschwitz physicians conducted actual physical examinations. Even though the physicians did not spend very long with each patient, there was at least some consensus as to the criteria needed for selection.

Dr. Horst Fischer was one of these physicians and attended several meetings that aimed to establish concrete selection parameters. Dr. Fischer explains how the criteria for selections were conducted:

> *There were several conferences of all ss physicians in Auschwitz to work out firm criteria for selections. These discussions produced essentially the following characteristics as prerequisites for the selections: starvation edemas; the complete lack of fatty tissue in the buttocks (to diagnose this the physicians had the naked inmates turn around); the suspicion of TB (because of the deficient medical equipment actual TB was difficult to diagnose, and it evidently seemed too bothersome to perform X rays in the main camp); accidents that caused broken bones; and severe suppuration. Roughly speaking, these were the cases in which selections appeared to be indicated.*

Examples of these cases were numerous in the infirmaries frequented by the slave labor force. As such, an SS physician did not have a difficult time finding those qualified for the gas chambers. One of the most senior physicians in the camp, Dr. Eduard Wirths, was consistently at odds with men such as Entress and Clauberg, among others. This was not due to Wirths" beneficence, as he is charged with removing the reproductive organs of large quantities of women without reason and without their consent. However, Wirths classified his experiments as true science, while he felt that Entress was simply a mad man. After requesting to be transferred out of the camp, Wirths decided to stay, and following this decision, the "lethal injections in the infirmaries were stopped. Entress and Klehr, were removed from their key positions, epidemics were brought under control; the supervision of nutrition was improved".

Wirths also entrusted more responsibility to inmate doctors, who were more sympathetic to their fellow prisoners. These actions did not cease his experiments, however, and following the war, Dr. Wirths committed suicide before he was brought to trial. Even with his heinous experiments, Wirths is remembered fondly by some SS and inmate physicians. Corruption in Auschwitz was endemic, with many SS men being bought off by items stolen from "Canada". These favors sometimes brought an extra ration of bread or saved an inmate from selection. Sometimes, inmates were even able to get the word out to loved ones across Europe or permitted to obtain a bottle of alcohol from the SS. Dr. Wirths, conversely, did not partake in the corruption. It is part of Wirths's personality profile that he and his family lived on his food ration coupons. In this, he was the lone exception in the jungle of corruption.

Dr. Wirths would not be considered one of the true and good "benevolent Nazis", but he was fondly remembered by many of those with whom he had daily contact. The stereotype of the SS officer as being cold, uneducated, and violent may not actually be true. Composed with an elite officer unit, the SS was comprised of men who came from educated and powerful families, and whose future was not solely tied to the military. Karl Brandt was the embodiment of this classification of leadership. Men such as Brandt were typically from an aristocratic or professional, often medical family whose general cultivation and pre-Nazi ethical concerns seemed strikingly at odds with the depth of his Nazi commitment.

Brandt became the personification of the educated Nazi, one who was worldly and well-read yet still bought into the machinations of systematic murder.

Karl Brandt was a powerful Nazi well before the founding of the Auschwitz concentration camp. He had become a commanding administrator in the Nazi Party, and in the autumn of 1939, Karl Brandt and Philipp Bouhler, head of the Chancellery of the Fuhrer, were personally entrusted by Hitler to organize and implement the "euthanasia" program. Brandt's participation in the euthanasia program increased, and he contributed to the first German case of killing a severely physically disabled newborn. The case is shrouded in mystery and the name of the child may never be known, but Brandt's involvement has been cataloged. Following the end of World War II, Brandt was taken into Allied custody and interrogated on his professional exploits and ethics. When the subject of euthanasia was broached, he spoke openly about the decisions behind Hitler's initiative to purify the German race.

Brandt's depositions propose that those who participated were not ignorant of the fact that their action was illegal. Hitler, Brandt even the parents knew that what they were doing was outside the law and generally accepted medical conduct. Brandt seemed to suffer no remorse resulting from his killing of the innocent child, a reaction which was validated soon thereafter, at the advent of 1940, when he participated in the first deadly injections in the adult "euthanasia" program.

The new ground had been broken about medical contributions in government-sanctioned killings, and Brandt was head of the new vanguard.

Karl Brandt was able to operate without fear of prosecution from the German government and this allowed him to lobby for an enlarged euthanasia program. Brandt, and his fellow SS elite, knew that their action was still against the law and contrary to medical ethics. As long as there was no official government legislation, they felt that their actions had to remain secret. Furthermore, those joining in the euthanasia initiative had a collective vested interest in keeping the program quiet.

While the German government may accommodate and approve of the initiative, most likely the same would not be said for the global community. Therefore, the euthanasia program spearheaded by Karl Brandt was kept relatively quiet and out of the public view. While in Allied custody, Brandt was routinely asked how he could reconcile his actions with his professional ethics. His explanation haunted the interrogators when he responded:

> *...doctors could not violate medical ethics, not because they were unable to inflict harm on humans, but because they were doctors. Their professional status freed them from any kind of moral and ethical responsibility towards their patients and gave them immunity from medical ethics violations.*

Brandt must have been fully indoctrinated in the Nazi beliefs to believe that doctors could not inflict harm on human beings, especially considering he was most likely well aware of the medical experiments occurring in horrific places such as Auschwitz. However, when pressed by his captors on this precise question, Brandt stood apart from the physicians of the concentration camps. Rather than showing a callous disregard for the life and dignity of subjects used for research in concentration camps... Brandt was largely indifferent to the ethics of human experimentation.

Brandt simply did not concern himself with ethical measures such as informed consent, do no harm, and other medical ethical principles. There were two main racial justifications for the establishment of concentration camps. The first justification was that the Jew was inherently evil and the staunch enemy of the European community, most especially the Aryan race. Therefore, the killing of Jews became not only acceptable but appropriate because it protected the life and rights of Aryans. The second justification is on more of a physical level: the non-material motive for getting a Jew to work was the satisfaction it gave his German masters, by providing them with the pleasing sight of a laboring Jew and by demonstrating their ability to subdue the Jew to such a degree that he acts contrary to his nature, namely like an honest man.... It fulfilled the psychological need, expressed again and again in German's treatment of Jews, to have total power over Jews.

The notion of total power extended itself to include power over the life and death of a Jewish prisoner. The evolution of Auschwitz from conception to killing center is an amazing journey. Auschwitz was not the first concentration camp, nor was it the first liquidation center for the undesirables. However, Auschwitz did become the most notorious concentration camp in the entire Third Reich and ultimately became the physical embodiment of the evil mankind can enact on each other. The survivor testimonials, which first emerged during the war but grew immensely following liberation, give insight into the daily horrors that a prisoner endured. It was not simply that an inmate had to avoid experimentation by one of the SS doctors, but also that the malnourished individual lived in constant fear of death at each moment in every day.

The location of Auschwitz was ideal for many reasons. First and foremost, it was not located in Germany, which Hitler had declared would be *judenfrei* (Jew-Free) by the end of 1941.

Furthermore, it would be located in the Polish countryside, an area which was easily masked by the creation of a buffer zone around the camp. Upon close examination the concentration camp inspectors saw its benefits: the area had transport connections, it was at a railway junction, and it was easy to close off against the outside world.

Finally, old Polish army barracks existed on the site of Auschwitz I and could be quickly converted to stone barracks which would provide housing for the labor force charged with building the remaining two subcamps. While Auschwitz I and Auschwitz III – Monowitz were the slave labor component to the entire Auschwitz operation, the primary function of Auschwitz was the murder of every single Jew the Nazis could (in Himmler's words) lay their hands on anywhere.

With transports arriving from nearly every corner of Europe, it became impossible to exterminate every individual immediately upon their arrival to Auschwitz, and so those selected as "fit to work" were transported away from Auschwitz II – Birkenau.

However, not every one of these new arrivals was physically able to work. Many were elderly or sick and they were accompanied by small children and pregnant mothers. The Nazis claimed they could not provide the sustenance necessary to keep the prisoners in good health; therefore the selection process was introduced. Indeed, Auschwitz, more than any other camp, reflected the inner Nazi struggle between pragmatic strengthening (through forced labor on war works) and visionary murder.

No matter how many prisoners were selected as "fit to work" or how many commodities were produced in Auschwitz III – Monowitz could hide the real function of Auschwitz. Auschwitz was created as the epicenter where the European Jews would be eliminated from existence.

The holding pen of Auschwitz II – Birkenau was not comprised entirely of Jews awaiting their turn in the gas chambers. It held vast numbers of nationalities and orientations and languages. Therefore, to keep order, a visible representation of one's identity was to be worn at all times. This identification was broken down as follows:

> *A system of identification was instituted, according to which each prisoner had a rectangular piece of material sewn onto his or her uniform, upon which was imprinted a colored triangle: red for political prisoners, purple for Jehovah's Witnesses, black for asocial (for example, prostitutes), green for criminals, and pink for homosexuals. Jews work a triangle (usually red), under which an added yellow triangle was sewn on to form a hexagram (Star of David).*

Those individuals seen without their identification were routinely tortured and exterminated. The sense of order was integral to the camp's structure. The reality now facing the new prisoners must have been quite confusing. In-home countries such as Greece, Italy, Czechoslovakia, Romania, among others, these human beings were packed into transport cars for the long journey to Poland, sometimes having to endure this dank and feces infested environment for days at a time. When one has been subject to that environment for such a period of time, any pretense regarding acceptable public behavior is eliminated. When the doors finally opened, the survivors, parched and overcome by thirst, threw themselves like unclean animals on the slimy water of the puddles lining the railroad tracks.

Sadly, this scene of starving and dehydrated inmates consuming any possible semblance of sustenance would be replayed daily in Auschwitz.

The loneliness of the new prisoners was debilitating. Following arrival, selection occurred, and those considered "fit to work" were separated from friends and family and simply ushered into the larger camp. Imagine now a man who is deprived of everything he loves, and at the same time of his house, his habits, his clothes, in short, of everything he possesses: he will be a hollow man, reduced to suffering and needs, forgetful of dignity and restraint, for he who loses all often easily loses himself.

The slide to the animalistic drive to survive began in earnest at this point. The new camp inductee was alone and subject to the camp's hierarchy, which may be conducted in a language this individual does not understand. For the Jewish inmates, it was worse. While the sending of letters was permitted for certain ethnicities and communal family camps existed for the Sinti and Roma (gypsies), the Jews were not granted any camp luxury. No word of the outside world, of family or friends, or the war effort ever made it into the Jewish district. As a people, they were alone and hunted by both the Nazis and fellow anti-Semitic inmates.

The camp itself was muddy and stagnant and had stagnant pools of blood adjacent to every bunk and walkway. The place was crawling with vermin; a constant lack of water made the situation worse, leading to epidemics such as spotted fever and typhus.

Bodies were sometimes left lying where the prisoner had died, and so decaying human flesh peppered the air with a heinous stench. The dehumanizing measures did not cease at that point. These individuals were led through the processing section of the camp where their identification numbers were tattooed on their arms, their bodies were shaved, and they were deloused before heading back into their new home. This process was entirely demeaning, especially for the women inmates: like all concentration camp inmates were deeply ashamed by the shaving on their bodies. Although men were less traumatized by these experiences than women, even they concurred that compulsory body shaving was just one of the many dehumanizing measures aimed at torturing all concentration camps prisoners. For women, it was much harder. Women"s sexual identification is more closely tied to their body and their hair. In concentration camps, public nudity and the shaving of body hair happened simultaneously.

The public shaming was soon followed by the donning of concentration camp garb, which was comprised of ill-fitting thin rags taken off the bodies of the recently deceased. The new arrival had precious little time to acclimate to the camp's structure.

New arrivals were assigned hard physical labor, whereas "old numbers" were more likely to get a good detail. The ss did not have to enforce this law rigorously, for it was respected by the inmate hierarchy. The reasoning for this included that the new arrival was likely in better shape to survive the grueling fifteen-hour workdays of hard labor. More importantly, though, it aided in breaking down the will of the prisoner.

Once that will is broken, the inmate becomes concerned only with the daily routine, and would not be interested in participating in an uprising. The skeletons that were the prisoner workforce became almost zombies, and a large percentage did not care if they lived or died.

If the new arrival sought the aid and support of experienced camp inmates, he or she was routinely denied even the simplest assistance: also, experienced inmates could hardly help someone who suffered the consequences of a shock. The fact that people in Auschwitz had few chances to think of matters that did not directly concern them was not the only reason. A host of informers made it risky to converse openly with someone whom one did not know well and who had as yet no camp experience. A thoughtless remark or reaction could mean mortal danger not only for the novice but also for his informant. Officially, an inmate was not supposed to know anything about the machinery of mass extermination, and talking about it was taboo. Precisely at the time when a helpless new arrival had the greatest need for support, he remained woefully isolated.

The new arrival was now completely and utterly alone. No support network was available, and fellow prisoners were concerned only with their own survival. Daily life in the Auschwitz concentration camp was nefarious and full of danger. The ever-present starvation made the day's sole focus amassing enough food to survive, and the experience of starvation was the cause of many of the camp's maladies. Lucie Adelsberger, an inmate doctor, explains that many despicable acts were perpetrated by prisoners. "...things that rightly seem outrageous and monstrous to the outsider, became understandable and to a certain extent excusable when seen from the perspective of starvation." These behaviors could include beating the weaker prisoners and stealing their rations or eating food encrusted with mold or feces.

Hermann Langbein addresses the reality of starvation by reporting how the Auschwitz survivor Judith Sternberg-Newman saw how her fellow prisoners "...stole bread from their dying comrades and ate it even if it was soiled by excrement. She confesses that she pulled a concealed bread ration from under the body of a woman who had just died."

This behavior was highly dangerous, as prisoners who were caught rummaging through the garbage for vestiges of food were severely beaten and denied their rations for a couple of days. Inmates suffering from starvation were required to attend daily roll calls, which sometimes lasted hours. During these roll calls, it was routine for an SS guard to perform selection and send the weakest of the group to the gas chambers. Due to this knowledge, the prisoners attempted every possible measure to ensure they looked healthier and stronger than the rest of the group. Some stuffed rags under their clothes to look fatter others rubbed whatever substance they could find on their faces to overcome pallor and produce color..."

It was routine to see groups of inmates jogging in place to produce color in their faces in hopes of appearing healthy. Hermann Langbein again writes that most prisoners had no illusions of enduring and surviving Auschwitz. However, the small modicum of hope still existed, that perhaps Providence would intervene and allow for the prisoner to survive.

Full immersion in death became an all too real life for Auschwitz's prisoners. Similar to how the SS men became desensitized to the horrors of the gas chambers, the prisoners became desensitized to seeing fellow inmates dying every day. It's amazing how a human being can adjust to living in terrible circumstances. You see a guy die – so what? I never thought of the man who was going to be hanged. I was ten or fifteen yards away from a life about to be snuffed out, and all I could think of was, "Let's get this over with so I can go back to the barracks and enjoy my free time." The most important thing was that I wasn't the man at the end of the rope.

Public executions were routinely employed by the SS as means of controlling the inmate population. However, after so much blood and death, some of the inmates became wholly unaffected by these actions. This desensitization is mirrored by Auschwitz survivor Hermann Langbein when he writes that he heard of a capo in the main camp demonstrating a new club grip to a colleague and "...called a Jew who happened to be passing by and used him to show how he could kill someone with one blow. The demonstration was successful. No one took notice of it."

While there may be time to mourn the death of a fellow inmate at a later date, assuming one was to survive; all human emotions must be suppressed in the interest of self-preservation.

Beatings were also a daily ritual in Auschwitz, following a very strict chain of command. The new arrivals were beaten by camp elders, the elders were beaten by capos, and the capos were beaten by the SS if the roll call numbers were not accurate, a commodity was missing, or if a member of the group was perceived as lazy. There are two examples that best characterize the daily beatings. The first is from a prisoner, Katarina Princz, who was interviewed after the war. Princz witnessed her block elder beating her own cousin nearly to death because the cousin, exhausted, had hidden during roll call.

The elder beat her cousin as a result of the beatings she received at the hands of the SS for being one number short. The second example also involves roll call:

> *Margit Teitelbaum was a dormitory elder in Block 23. One day someone from her barracks was missing at the roll call, and the ss was furious. It turned out that a Jewish woman from Holland had hidden in a pallet. Since Teitelbaum was responsible for all inhabitants in her barracks, she was given twenty-five lashes on her behind with a whip in front of all those assembled. The Dutch woman was shot.*

Routine beatings became a way for SS guards to instill order and capitulation amongst the prisoner population. No inmate, no matter the relationship with a camp elder or capo or how corrupt the SS guard allowed himself to be, was immune to this threat.

The smokestacks of the crematorium stood as a constant reminder to each and every inmate that their lives could end in a manner of minutes.

For those unlucky souls who entered the gas chamber, it was undoubtedly a harrowing experience. Now everyone has undressed. Pitiful skeletons. Their numbers are taken down, and they are chased into the block. The sun is shining, and the snow is glistening and merrily dripping from the roof. No one is in front of my window; all I can see are big piles of dirty prison clothes along the wall. Then I hear footsteps and muted voices from the corridor. I look outside. Now there are long lines of naked inmates. The clerk of our block walks up to each one with file cards in his hand, compares names and numbers, and writes each inmate's number on their chests; these inmates are already counted among the dead, and there has to be order.

The surreal vision of bright skies and shining snow placed against the backdrop of so much murder and suffering is unfathomable. There is a difference, however, between those committed to the gas chambers after surviving in Auschwitz for a certain period of time and those who were led to the gas chambers immediately after departing the transport cars. The SS took extreme measures to trick the Jews emerging from the train from start to finish. During deportation from their home countries, they were permitted to bring luggage and personal items, as they were being resettled in a new Jewish establishment in the East.

Furthermore, certain SS administrators sold plots of land to the Jews, where they would be able to build a new home and a new life once they arrived. Once the Jews arrived at Auschwitz, the trickery continued. The gas chambers were equipped with showerheads to fuel the deception. The SS guards told the prisoners that following disinfection, they would be reunited with their loved ones, and oftentimes SS men told the walking dead that coffee and cakes would be available after the showers.

The scene was as follows:

> *On the steps leading to the changing room there hung a panel, in German, French, Greek, and Hungarian, showing the arrivals the way to the "bathroom" and the "disinfection room." Benches and numbered clothes-hooks in the changing room suggested that the prisoners would be returning to their personal effects. Here there were also panels bearing such mottoes as "One louse – your death" and "Through cleanliness to freedom." On the door to the gas chamber it said "Bath and disinfection room," and from the ceiling hung sieves mounted on pieces of wood, to look like showerheads. Sometimes the SS handed out soap and towels before they shut the gas chambers, each holding up to 2,000 people.*

Once inside the showers, an SS man trained to handle the Zyklon-B would deposit the poison, and both SS Doctors and SS soldiers were able to watch the macabre scene inside the showers through specially designed peepholes. For the inmates who had lived and suffered in Auschwitz proper for a period of time, each knew full well what lies at the end of the stairs. For some, resistance was paramount, and beatings were soon to follow. For others, they simply followed orders and proceeded into the chambers unaffected.

The rule was that the inmates, being exhausted unto death, an apathetic mass, let themselves be directed wherever the all-powerful ss pleased.

For some this was a form of suicide and others had simply lost all hope of survival. To blame the victims for not resisting the march into the gas chambers is inappropriate, as one cannot comprehend the starvation, beatings, blood, and murder that these inmates experienced on a minute by minute basis, and therefore one cannot understand how that experience can completely break a person.

There was, however, one major cause of resistance. The Sonderkommando was a special unit mainly comprised of Jews who were responsible for the disposal of corpses. Following the gas chambers duties, this group would remove the corpses and load each body into the ovens. On days where the ovens were overworked, the bodies were stacked into trenches and burned. It was an occupation where the prisoners saw untold amounts of death, sometimes of even relatives and friends. The author and activist Elie Wiesel arrived in Auschwitz in 1944, alongside his friend Bela Katz. "Later Katz sent word to his friend that he had been assigned to the *Sonderkommando*, where he was forced to push his own father into the gas chamber." It is reasonable to assume that Bela Katz later had to push his dead father"s body into the ovens and watch as it slowly turned to ash.

The *Sonderkommando* were always working on borrowed time. As witnesses to the most violent atrocities committed by the Nazis at Auschwitz, each *Sonderkommando* group was itself liquidated after two or three months. Towards the end of the war, when the Nazi defeat was imminent, this knowledge prompted one of the last *Sonderkommando* groups to stage a rebellion with the assistance of the Polish underground.

The uprising commenced as follows:

An SS prisoner selection finally prompted the uprising: after an attempted escape the SS had murdered 200 members of the *Sonderkommando* with cyanide in a storage room used for personal effects. Three hundred further prisoners were to follow, and it was the responsibility of the *Sonderkommandos* of crematoria IV and V to make the selections. When, on the morning of 7 October 1944, the SS announced that those selected were to be transferred o another camp the same day, the same message as had been given to the prisoners murdered in the past, the uprising broke out: just before half-past one in the afternoon prisoners attacked approaching SS men in crematorium IV with stones, axes and iron bars, set the building on fire with smuggled hand-grenades and fled. The smoke alarmed the prisoners in the other crematoria. The SS set up machine-guns in crematorium IV and fired into the crowd of prisoners; those who were not hit immediately were forced into crematorium V, which faced crematorium IV.

The rebellion spread to crematorium II, where the prisoners managed to part the barbed wire and flee, at least temporarily. Beyond the "outer cordon" some made it to the adjacent forests, and others to the fish-breeding plants and agricultural estates in Rajsko, where they were able to arm themselves and attack the SS. Some of them hid in a barn, where they were locked in and burned alive.

While none of the rebels survived the uprising, the rebellion was successful in destroying the crematoria in an act of defiance. Not soon thereafter, as a result of the advancing Russian Red Army, the gas chamber operations were ceased. It is reasonable to assume the Sonderkommando activity played a part in shutting down the gassings as well, as Auschwitz no longer could murder on such a grand level.

In summation, the terrible environment of Auschwitz extended far beyond Josef Mengele. It was a horrific setting in a desolation location and became the most notorious death factory of the Second World War. While Josef Mengele does not solely define Auschwitz, he is certainly indicative of the Nazis' Final Solution.

CHAPTER VII

CONCLUSIONS

Josef Mengele does not, by himself, encompass the atrocities committed at the Auschwitz concentration camp. He is, however, widely considered the most infamous Nazi doctor employed anywhere within the Third Reich. Before researching this book, I was aware of Mengele's reputation as a gruesome and evil doctor but was not cognizant of his specific activities. In an attempt to unlock the programmability of genetics, Josef Mengele experimented and operated on countless victims, mainly children. He eschewed his professional and social ethics in an attempt to advance his academic career and relished the power he held over the prisoners of Auschwitz.

Analyzing and documenting Mengele's scientific research was emotionally draining, but I am glad to have had the experience. Furthermore, in conclusion, Josef Mengele's experiments were so heinous and so evil that no good could ever have come from his trials. No matter how one assesses Mengele's pseudo-scientific merit or analyzes his results through an ethical spectrum, only one conclusion can be reached.

This author strongly believes that the research conducted by Josef Mengele was professionally and philosophically unethical, and any use of his results would likewise be impermissible.

The human experiments in German concentration camps did not just conjure out of thin air. The developments in modern medicine, including the rise of new research fields such as pharmacology and bacteriology, made experiments on humans necessary. Germany was by no means the only country where scientists and physicians used human bodies for the improvement in medical knowledge and the development of new medicines and treatments.

At the end of the nineteenth- and the beginning of the twentieth century, human experiments became a common practice in medicine in almost all civilized and industrialized countries. In many cases, people were used as research subjects without their informed consent, particularly poor hospitalized persons, mentally ill patients in asylums, and people living in the European colonies. These cases remained largely unknown to the public. Only experiments that caused the death of the research subjects received public attention.

The social and political crisis after the First World War intensified the emergence of racial hygiene in Germany and led to a shift in focus for medicine from the individual to the community. The healing of the ill *Volkskörper* based on racial principles became the highest aim. The racially pure and healthy life became more valuable than the racially degenerated one. Physicians became the physiological engineers of the society. They aimed to heal the national body. Racial hygiene created a framework in which physicians regarded human bodies in terms of usefulness for the benefit of society. If necessary, useless bodies could be sacrificed for the creation of a racially pure nation. The doctors determined which life was useful or useless. Nevertheless, racial hygiene should be considered as a continuation of medicine based on natural science methods that developed in the nineteenth century. The same is valid for human experiments. The National Socialist state offered physicians research subjects; useless bodies, that could contribute to the future welfare of the German nation.

However, the mental framework of using bodies for scientific progress in medicine already existed well before the Third Reich.

German doctors played a crucial role in the implementation of Nazi racial policies, such as the Nuremberg racial laws, the sterilization of mentally and chronically ill patients, and the euthanasia program. The Nazis did not confiscate German medicine or deceive German physicians. Doctors themselves willingly chose to collaborate with the new state. They did so out of opportunistic reasons. The doctors became members of the NSDAP, SA, and SS because these organizations could advance their careers. Particularly in the SS, doctors were overrepresented as a profession.

The Third Reich brought the doctors career improvements. The new state created many jobs and the exclusion of Jewish scientists further opened up the possibilities for German physicians, who received better positions, a rise in income, and consequently a higher social status. Some of the older doctors received a professorship during the Nazi era.

The younger generation built their careers out of their membership of the SS. They could quickly make a career in the Third Reich and would opportunistically exploit the opportunities that the concentration camps offered them during the war.

The outbreak of the war against the Soviet Union and the subsequent implementation of the Holocaust prompted the large-scale human experiments in German concentration camps. The genocidal mindset devalued every form of inferior life. The lives of individuals became worthless because they could simply be replaced. With every legal and ethical boundary omitted, anything became possible. Besides the immediate elimination of these useless bodies, their only function was to serve as research subjects to contribute to the survival of the National Socialist state and the German people. Before the war, researchers only executed small-scale experiments on inmates. In contrast to this previous human experimentation, the death of the research subjects was now integrated into the research design. The authorities that initiated the experiments and the doctors immediately realized the unlimited opportunities. Consequently, they started making preparations and asked for formal approval. Thus, most of the experiments came into being in the year 1942.

After the war, the Nazi doctors defended their actions by exonerating arguments. However, as the prosecutors and judges argued, none of these arguments legitimized the involuntary use of prisoners. None of the Nazi doctors felt guilty for their crimes. They believed that they had done what was right. Their normative reference frame based on National Socialism explains their mind-set and this perspective. The Nazi doctors had no ethical and moral constraints to executing the human experiments because they deemed the lives of the research subjects as inferior and useless.

The perpetrators of human experiments were not monsters or pseudo-scientists. They were intelligent researchers and scientists. They supported National Socialism and racial hygiene out of ideological and opportunistic reasons. The ambition to build an academic career or discover a scientific breakthrough was their motive to either actively seek or to willingly accept the unique opportunity offered by the National Socialist state.

There seems to be a contradiction between the top-down structure and the eager and ambitious doctors. However, this can be explained. Human experiments were a common practice in medicine and supported by doctors. Before the war, the moral values of the society concerning human experimentation, expressed by the movement for legal guidelines, restricted the use of humans as research subjects. Although almost every physician opposed these moral and legal restrictions, they had to abide by them. The public did not accept any medical experiments without the informed consent of the research subjects, let alone any deaths. This limited the possibilities in the medical research of doctors and scientists. The Nazi doctors realized that the approval by the state to execute these kinds of experimentation in a secret setting was a unique opportunity.

Thus, the state only had to allow human experimentation to attract the attention of doctors. The state provided the necessary resources and the doctors willingly seized the opportunity. In seizing this opportunity, they did not have any ethical and moral constraints whatsoever.

Don't miss out!

Visit the website below and you can sign up to receive emails whenever Jack Stew Barretta publishes a new book. There's no charge and no obligation.

https://books2read.com/r/B-A-RLUP-QNASB

BOOKS 2 READ

Connecting independent readers to independent writers.

Also by Jack Stew Barretta

The Black Death and The Medical Practice How The Plague Pandemic Influenced Medicine and Surgery
The Black Death and his Unexpected Positive Consequences to Society
Auschwitz Children and Mengele Experiments The Immoral and Atrocious Research on Children in the Auschwitz Concentration Camp During World War II

Milton Keynes UK
Ingram Content Group UK Ltd.
UKHW022237050124
435526UK00015B/571

9 798215 199732